THE FROG WITH SELF-CLEANING FEET

THE FROG WITH SELF-CLEANING FEET

... AND OTHER EXTRAORDINARY TALES FROM THE ANIMAL WORLD

MICHAEL BRIGHT

Skyhorse Publishing
A Herman Graf Book

First published in Great Britain in 2012 by The Robson Press (an imprint of Biteback Publishing Ltd.), Westminster Tower, 3 Albert Embankment, London SE1 7SP.

Skyhorse Publishing books may be purchased in bulk at special discounts for sales promotion, corporate gifts, fund-raising, or educational purposes. Special editions can also be created to specifications. For details, contact the Special Sales Department, Skyhorse Publishing, 307 West 36th Street, 11th Floor, New York, NY 10018 or info@skyhorsepublishing.com.

Skyhorse® and Skyhorse Publishing® are registered trademarks of Skyhorse Publishing, Inc.®, a Delaware corporation.

Visit our website at www.skyhorsepublishing.com.

10 9 8 7 6 5 4 3 2 1

Library of Congress Cataloging-in-Publication Data is available on file.

ISBN: 978-1-62636-075-4

Printed in the United States of America

CONTENTS

INTRODUCTION

Since we shared our caves with other animals, we have been fascinated by what they do and how they relate to us; these beasts of the field, fowl of the air and fish of the sea never fail to surprise us. The ancients painted images of the more familiar animals on their cave walls, worshipped them, tamed them and ate them. Nowadays we study them (and eat them and pollute them into oblivion), but whatever we do to them, somehow most of them keep bouncing back. This miscellany of animal stories might offer a few reasons why.

Take the frog with the self-cleaning feet. White's tree frog *Litoria caerulea*, named after the English surgeon and botanist John White (c.1756–1832), produces sticky mucus on the bottom of its feet at every step. Channels on the bottom of the feet leave dirt behind and new mucus is secreted in its place, so the frog's feet are always clean. And we can learn from this remarkable creature: researchers believe this could lead to self-cleaning bandages and self-renewing adhesives.

In fact, frogs, and their warty relatives the toads, are amazing animals. While most frogs swim, there are few that fly. Wallace's flying frog *Rhacophorus nigropalmatus* uses the webbing between its toes like four tiny parachutes and glides safely to the ground or an adjacent tree. Then there are the jumpers, like the rocket frog *Litoria nasuta*, which can make 2-metre (6.6ft) leaps by storing energy in its tendons and releasing it suddenly to enhance the performance of its muscles. Spadefoot toads have a hard extension on their hind feet, like tiny pick axes, that help them burrow, digging backwards into the ground. The wrinkly Lake Titicaca frog *Telmatobius culeus* does push-ups on the lake bed to increase the flow of water around its body to gain more oxygen in an oxygen-depleted environment. The Bornean flat-headed frog *Barbourula kalimantanensis* breathes without a lung and the wood frog *Rana sylvatica* freezes almost solid in winter. But, that's enough about frogs.

This little book includes stories from across the animal kingdom: the honeypot ants *Myrmecocystus mendax* that become living storage jars; the barnacles *Amphibalanus amphitrite* which stick to rocks with a glue that hardens in the same way human blood clots; the leaf beetles *Gastrophysa viridula* which have no fewer than three types of tiny hairs on the bottom of their feet, each with a different 'stickiness' and a different function; and a shocking pink centipede *Desmoxytes purpurosea* ... yes, shocking pink!

Then, there are the things nature invented first: the chemical 'chitosan' in crab shells that might lead to a paint that actually heals itself – instant scratch repair on your car; the three-layered shell of an Indian Ocean deep-sea snail *Crysomallon squamiferum* that could give rise to better body armour for the military; sea urchin teeth that are designed to stay sharp; and the flippers of humpback whales *Megaptera novaeangliae* that have features being drafted in to the design of more efficient ocean turbine blades and helicopter blades.

And who'd have thought that juvenile birds could be scared to an early death just by hearing a predator; that female short-finned pilot whales *Globicephala macrorhynchus* are one of the few animals that go through the menopause like humans; or that wolves howl in harmony to give the impression the pack is bigger than it really is?

All these things are real. You couldn't make them up. These animals have been observed, recorded and reported in scientific journals during the first decade of the twenty-first century. This book extracts the latest and most intriguing stories from the scientific world and presents them in short 'bites' of easy to digest animal trivia. There are the record-breakers, the most deadly, the most venomous, the largest and smallest, loudest and quietest, fastest and slowest, many of which are species new to science. Then there are the highest flyers and the deepest divers, the cheats and those in the protection racket, the smart and not so smart, and the tool-users. And, to focus a little on the fun and the frivolous, I've included lists of nicknames and oddball scientific names, and tracked down all those unusual collective names.

This is a book in which to dip in and out of, and I hope you find the stories as entertaining, informative and mind-blowing as I have.

To include the primary sources of all these tales would fill a book in itself, so for those who would like to follow up any stories that you read here, you can find a list of sources at my website www.michaelbright.co.uk

WHAT'S IN A (SCIENTIFIC) NAME?

All living things have a scientific name in at least two parts – the genus and the species, and they are printed in italics, e.g. *Homo sapiens*, meaning 'wise man'. The two words should indicate some of the properties of an organism or where it was found or who found it, or be named in honour of somebody, e.g. *Zaglossus attenboroughi* – Sir David's long-beaked echidna. On the face of it, taxonomy – the scientific discipline of classification – seems a somewhat 'dry' subject, but there you'd be wrong. Taxonomists have a sense of humour. Take a look at these:

Montypythonoides riversleighensis is a giant fossil snake that was discovered at Riversleigh, Queensland, Australia.

Arthurdactylus conan-doylensis is a pterodactyl named after the author of *The Lost World*.

Dracorex hogwartsia is a dinosaur found in South Dakota, whose name means 'the dragon king of Hogwarts'.

Eucritta melanolimnetes is an early tetrapod fossil discovered in Scotland whose name means 'true creature of the Black Lagoon'.

Ichabodcraniosaurus is a velociraptor-like dinosaur fossil that was found in Mongolia without its skull and named after Ichabod Crane, a character in Washington Irving's *The Legend of Sleepy Hollow*. In the story, a headless horseman chased Crane.

Ytu brutus is a 2mm (0.079in.) long water beetle from Brazil and for *The Matrix* fans there's *Ytu morpheus*.

Ba humbugi is a Pacific land snail from Mba Island, Fiji; *Agra phobia* and *Agra vation* are carabid beetles from the South American rainforest; and *Hunkydora* and *Abra cadabra* are clams (sadly, *A. cadabra* has been renamed *Theora*).

The primitive fish fossils *Ptomaspis*, *Dikenaspis* and *Ariaspis* represent Tom, Dick and Harry, and there are the palindromes for the syrphid fly *Xela alex,* the scarab beetle *Orizabus subaziro* and a genus of molluscs *Allenella*.

Peiza pi, Peiza rhea, Peiza kake, Peiza deresistans, Phthiria relativitae and *Ohmyia omya* are all flies.

Eubetia bigaulae, pronounced 'youbetchabygolly' and *Eubetia boop* are tortricid moths.

Heerz lukenatcha, Heerz tooya, Verae peculya, and *Panama canalia* are braconid wasps.

Gelae baen, Gelae belae, Gelae donut, Gelae fish and *Gelae rol* are all tiny brown beetles that live in fungi.

Cyclocephala nodanotherwon is a scarab beetle and *Cephise nuspesez* is a new species of skipper butterfly.

Apopyllus now and *Draculoides bramstokeri* are spiders, and *Walckenaeria pinocchio* is a spider with a long nose.

Eurygenius and *Oops* are genera of beetles, and *Notoreas* is a genus of moths.

Erechthias beeblebroxi is a false-headed moth and *Fiordichthys slartibartfasti* is a triple-fin blenny (fish), both of which pay homage to Douglas Adams's *The Hitchhiker's Guide to the Galaxy*.

Pericompus bilbo is a short, fat carabid beetle with hairy feet, reminiscent of J. R. R. Tolkien's *The Hobbit*.

Gressitia titsadaysi and *Tabanus rhizonshine* are horseflies, and *Rhyacophila tralala* is a caddis fly.

Vini vidivici is the conquered lorikeet from the South Pacific, and *Castnia inca dincadu* is a castiid moth.

Ittibitium is a genus of molluscs that are smaller than the genus *Bittium*.

In 1912, English entomologist George Kirkaldy came in for a bit of stick from the grandees of the London Zoological Society after he named a collection of true bugs with words that sounded like 'kiss me', together with the names of girlfriends. There was *Ochisme* ('Oh kiss me'), *Dollichisme* ('Dolly kiss me'), *Florichisme* ('Flori kiss me'), *Marichisme* ('Mary kiss me'), *Nanichisme* ('Nanie kiss me') and *Polychisme* ('Polly kiss me').

And there was worse to come. Some of the ruder binomial names – look away now – include: *Batrachuperus longdongensis*, a salamander from the Longdong River in the Sichuan Province of China; *Chrysops balzaphire*, a deer fly; *Bugeranus carunculatus*, the wattled crane, the largest crane in Africa; *Enema pan* is a rhinoceros beetle from South America; *Fartulum* spp. is a genus of sausage-shaped gastropod molluscs; *Turdus* is a genus of birds that are true thrushes; *Poospiza* is a genus of warbling finches from South America; *Pison eu* is an apoid wasp; and *Eremobates inyoanus* is a camel spider that was first found in Inyo County, California.

And finally, from 1927, there's the world's longest binomial name. It was proposed for an amphipod from Lake Baikal in Russia, but wasn't accepted and never made it to the text books – what a pity:

Gammaracanthuskytodermogammarus loricato baicalensis.

SMART ANIMALS

Even with a 'brain' one-millionth the size of the human brain, paper wasps of the genus *Polistes* not

5

only recognise the faces of others of their kind, much like we do, but also remember those individuals and related events for at least a week.

Like people pointing with their finger, ravens *Corvus corax* gesture with their beaks to attract attention and point out objects to one other. In this way, they will offer moss, stones and twigs to other ravens.

A captive elephant *Elephas maximus* called Happy who lives in New York's Bronx Zoo, recognised herself in a mirror and, watching her reflection, she manipulated her trunk and her ear. She joins an elite group of animals, including humans, other apes and dolphins in being able to recognise 'self'.

Rats *Rattus* appear to feel and respond to each other's distress and will try to release another rat caught in a trap.

Abstract concepts, such as counting, is an ability we generally reserve for our nearest primate relatives and ourselves, but now pigeons *Columba livia* have shown they can count too. They can place a number of images in numerical order depending on the number of objects in the picture.

The gloomy octopus *Octopus tetricus*, which lives in Sydney harbour, is a sophisticated viewer. It ignores anything on standard definition televisions, but reacts to the detailed images on high-definition sets. It'll move forward to catch a crab on the screen and back off when another octopus appears, just as it would do in the wild. However, it seems to have 'moods'. One day the octopus will react to HD video of a crab scuttling across the screen, but the next day it'll show little interest. Gloomy octopuses have, according to researchers at Australia's Macquarie University, 'episodic personalities'.

TOOL USERS

In the wild, New Caledonian crows *Corvus moneduloides* whittle hooks from twigs to winkle out grubs in the ground, while in the laboratory 'Betty', the New Caledonian crow, has manufactured a 'hook' from a piece of straight wire to lift a food reward from the bottom of a pot.

In Japan, crows *Corvus* wait for cars to stop at traffic lights and then drop walnuts they've collected onto the road before the lights turn green again. The cars drive over the nuts and crack them, and at the next red light the crows swoop down to collect the mashed up kernels. Gulls sometimes drop oysters on roads for the same reason.

Green herons *Butorides virescens* in North America have been seen to place feathers and pieces of biscuit on the water surface to catch any fish that come to investigate, and a European bittern *Botaurus stellaris* was once seen to drop insects on the water as bait to catch a meal.

The brown-headed nuthatch *Sitta pusilla* in southeastern USA holds a piece of bark in its bill to dig for insects. The woodpecker finch *Camarhynchus pallidus* in the Galapagos Islands uses a cactus spine to winkle out grubs, and the Egyptian vulture *Neophron percnopterus* uses rocks to crack open ostrich eggs.

The orange-dotted tuskfish *Choerodon anchorago* digs clams from the sandy seabed and carries his prize to a suitable rock where he cracks the shells by repeatedly smashing them against his chosen anvil. Other species of wrasse, a family of often brightly coloured marine fish, including the blackspot tuskfish *C. schloenleinii* on the Great Barrier Reef and the yellowhead wrasse *Halichoeres garnoti* on the Florida coast, have also been seen using an anvil.

Sea otters *Enhydra lutris* off the coast of the Pacific Northwest use a hammer and anvil. The hammer is a 'favourite' stone that they carry under their arm, and they smash it against sea urchins or clams which they rest on their stomachs while floating on their backs.

In Shark Bay, Western Australia, bottlenose dolphins *Tursiops aduncus* protect their sensitive snouts with pieces of natural sponge when foraging on the sea floor, and will spend some time finding a piece of sponge that fits, like a glove over a hand. The sponge is used to scatter the abrasive sand in the search for buried fish. If one is found, the dolphin drops the sponge and sets off in pursuit. The dolphins go to all this bother because bottom-dwelling species, especially the barred sandperch *Parapercis nebulosa* – a favourite with some Shark Bay dolphins – are more nutritious than open-water fish.

In the Bahamas, spotted dolphins *Stenella frontalis* search for fish under much softer sand using echolocation. This is because their prey species have swim bladders, an organ that helps to maintain buoyancy, which reflect their echolocation signals. Australia's barred sandperch don't have swim bladders and the seabed is not nearly so soft, so the dolphins have adopted this novel way of probing for a meal.

Dolphins sometimes catch fish, not with fishing rods or nets, but with large seashells. In Shark Bay, some individuals are seen to throw conch shells out of the water and shake them violently. Observers thought they were simply playing; that is, until biologists from Murdoch University took a picture of one and discovered it was swallowing a fish from the shell. Apparently, the dolphin chases the fish into an empty conch shell and stuns it by batting the shell around. Then, it upends the shell and the fish slips out, right into the dolphin's mouth, and is swallowed like a gourmet slurping an oyster.

Common chimpanzees *Pan troglodytes* don't just use tools, they have complete tool-kits. When eating ants, observed field biologists with the Goualougo Triangle Ape Project, the chimps have a tool to perforate the nest and a dipping tool to extract the ants. If they used their hands to excavate the nest, the ants would swarm out and inflect painful bites, but by using a small digging tool they localise the exodus and collect the ants that swarm up the dipping stick. Chimps also like honey and again they have an appropriate tool-kit. They use clubs to gain access to the tree nests of bees, and then fashion a different-shaped dipping stick. They fray the end of a twig by biting it with the teeth, which better picks up the honey, a bit like a spoon.

Other chimpanzee troops and bonobos *Pan paniscus* use scrunched-up leaves as a sponge to obtain water from tree hollows. Gorillas and orangutans have been seen to use a stick to check the depth of water in the river they were about to cross, with one gorilla using a stick to support itself as it crossed.

Chimpanzees in Africa and capuchin monkeys *Cebus* in South America use rocks to break open nuts, and capuchins use stones to dig up tubers and sticks to flush animals from rock crevices.

Each morning at Fongoli, in eastern Senegal, chimpanzees drop from their night nests in the trees and spend most of their day foraging across the savannah much as early humans must have done. Using their teeth, they fashion spears from sticks to harpoon bush babies in tree hollows and catch bushbuck fawns. They 'fish' for termites using a piece of saba vine and eat the saba fruit, up to thirty a day when in season. They visit parts of their huge home range, ten times bigger than that of rainforest chimps, when particular foods are ready to eat, much as someone in a giant supermarket knows where each commodity is to be found. They

THE FROG WITH SELF-CLEANING FEET

will share not only meat but also plant foods, honey and tools. In the afternoon, they might while away the hottest part of the day in a cool cave or soak in a cooling waterhole. And, they end the day by preparing a comfortable nest for the night ... just like we do.

CUNNING BUGS

A South American species of assassin bug *Salyavata variegata* eats termites, and it catches them in a unique way. First, it covers itself with pieces of the termites' nest as camouflage and heads for the entrance. There, it impales a termite on its sharp snout and sucks it dry. Then the bug grabs the empty exoskeleton and dangles it in front of the entrance, jiggling it a bit to attract attention. When a worker termite comes to dispose of the dead body, the assassin bug grabs it and sucks it dry too; and so it goes on, until the bug has consumed about thirty termites. It then leaves to digest its meal. This is the first known example of an insect using a tool, in this case, a bait, to capture prey.

In Australia, another assassin bug *Stenolemus bituberus* sneaks up on a spider in its web and then dupes it by mimicking prey caught in a web. It plucks the web's silk threads in a very precise way. When a fly is caught in a spider's web it struggles violently and the spider comes running to subdue it; if it is small prey or it has been in the web for a while, it tires and the movements are less violent, so the spider is less aggressive and not in a hurry. It's these smaller vibrations that the assassin bug mimics. The spider approaches nonchalantly with the expectation of a tasty morsel but, instead, it becomes the hapless victim before it has time to react. The assassin bug stabs it and sucks it dry. But the bugs don't have everything their own way. Spiders are also resourceful predators and sometimes the bug gets its comeuppance.

THE CHEATS

The tongue-eating louse *Cymothoa exigua* devours the tongue of its fish host and then replaces it with itself, so it is sitting in a prime spot in the fish's mouth to intercept anything that its host catches – and the fish seems quite unaware that it no longer has a tongue!

The white-winged shrike-tanager *Lanio versicolor* is a sentinel for mixed flocks of antbirds that follow columns of the army ants *Eciton*. They feed on the insects flushed out by the ants. If a bird-eating hawk appears, the sentinel emits an alarm call and all the birds dive for cover. However, if the shrike and a bird of another species are pursuing the same insect, the shrike gives a false alarm call. The other bird hears the alarm and hesitates momentarily, so the shrike catches the prey.

South American tufted capuchin monkeys *Cebus apella nigritus* are devious too. They live in a hierarchical society of groups of between seven and forty animals, with the dominant animals having first access to the best feeding sites. Monkeys further down the pecking order, however, have found a way to cheat their elders and betters. When a high-ranking individual is about to pick up a choice piece of food, the subordinate one gives the hiccup-like alarm call. The dominant one runs for cover and the low-ranking monkey grabs the food.

A silverfish *Malayatelura ponerophila* (related to the silvery insects found in bathrooms) lives with army ants *Leptogenys distinguenda* in Malaysia. It covers itself with ant odour so they do not attack it. The silverfish rubs the scent from defenceless young ants, known as 'callows', so it can roam about the nest unmolested and steal the ants' food.

Carnivorous female fireflies *Photuris* flash mate-attracting signals of another species *Photinus* to lure males looking for would-be mates. The unsuspecting males get more than they bargained for – their tryst ends in death.

On the savannah of East Africa, the male topi *Damaliscus korrigum* tries to keep a female on heat in his territory by pretending there is a predator nearby. As the female antelope starts to leave, he runs in front of her, stands stock still, staring into the distance, and then snorts. The snort is an alarm call, but this time it's a fake one. The female runs back into his territory and he mates with her almost immediately.

A female plover (Family: Charadiidea) adopts a 'broken-wing' display. This feigning of an injury distracts a predator away from her nest. The bird encourages it to follow her rather than find her eggs or chicks.

The margay *Leopardus wiedii*, a South American wild cat, mimics the calls of its prey in order to entice it into catching range. Researchers from the Federal University of Amazonas made the observation, the first record of a New World cat behaving in this way, although hunters' tales point to jaguars and pumas doing so too. On this occasion, the margay mimicked pied tamarins, a squirrel-sized monkey of the tropical rainforest. The sentinel monkey, along with a couple of others in the troop, were sufficiently intrigued to investigate the familiar yet slightly strange version of their call. They clambered down the tree towards the tangle of lianas from where the sound was coming. At that point, the margay appeared, but the sentinel was alert and screeched an alarm call. The tamarins scattered. The ruse hadn't worked this time, but the researchers were struck by the margay's ingenuity.

The caterpillar of Europe's large blue butterfly *Phengaris arion* is the ultimate deceiver. It produces a sugary substance that encourages red ants *Myrmica sabuleti* to take it back to their nest. It dupes the ants into believing it is one of their own by making the minute sounds that a queen ant emits, so it is fed and tended just like the queen. If the nest is disturbed the ants will carry the caterpillar to a safe place, giving it preferential treatment as if it is a queen, and ignoring their own larvae. During pupation, the butterfly pupa continues to make the sounds inside its chrysalis so it is still protected, and when the adult butterfly emerges, the ants even escort it to the surface, guarding it while its wings dry. It then flies away.

THE PROTECTION RACKET

Fork-tailed drongos *Dicrurus adsimilis* in South Africa are in the protection racket. They take care of flocks of pied babblers *Turdoides bicolor* by watching out for predators, which enables the babblers to spread out and feed without having to look up so often. The drongos occasionally earn their keep by spotting danger, giving real alarm calls and mobbing aerial predators, but actually they live up to their reputation as gangsters. They give false alarm calls, stealing food from right under the noses of the babblers while they're momentarily distracted, but the babblers put up with this: it's the price they pay for protection. Even so, the babblers are much more responsive to alarm calls from other babblers in their flock. Like any protection racket, those that are victimised do not trust their so-called 'protectors' entirely.

Brown-headed cowbirds *Molothrus ater* in North America behave like Mafiosi. They deposit their eggs in the nests of other birds – nest parasitism – but if a host bird, such as a warbler, rejects the cowbird's eggs, its nest is totally destroyed. The retaliation encourages potential hosts to accept and nurture the cowbird's offspring. In experiments by researchers from the University of Florida, it was found that 56 per cent of 'rejector' nests were destroyed compared to only 6 per cent of nests of 'accepter' birds. And, when the host birds rebuilt their nests, 85 per cent were re-parasitised by cowbirds, and the alien eggs accepted. The host birds appear to have learned to accept the cowbird's eggs, for not to do so would result in 60 per cent fewer host offspring. Intimidation, it seems, pays handsomely for mafia cowbirds.

TONGUES

The animal with the world's largest tongue is, not unexpectedly, the blue whale *Balaenoptera musculus*. Its tongue weighs around 2.7 tonnes, the same as a Land Rover Discovery 3.

The tongue of the chameleon (Family: Chamaeleonidae), which can be longer than the animal's body, is a complex arrangement of muscle and bone. When catching prey, a bone at the base of the tongue moves forward rapidly, providing the momentum for the rest of the elasticated tongue to shoot out faster than the human eye can see and hit the target in three-hundredths of a second. At the tip is a muscular club coated with mucus, which forms a suction cup. The prey sticks to the mucus and the tongue drawn back into the mouth. The tongue also works well in all weathers. It does not slow down like the rest of the chameleon's body in cold weather, enabling the chameleon to catch food at a greater temperature range than other lizards.

The tongue of a frog (Order: Anura) is attached at the front of the mouth rather than at the back, like ours. It is about a third of the frog's body length and can shoot out to catch a fly at fifteen-hundredths of a second. It works like a catapult. At rest, the tongue muscles are flaccid, but the moment prey is spotted fibres down the middle of the tongue stiffen, giving the tongue a rod-like rigidity. Muscles perpendicular to the base of the tongue contract rapidly, propelling it up, around and out of the mouth. The end splats into the prey like a sticky wet dishcloth and other muscles pull everything back into the mouth ... and all in the blink of an eye.

In southern Canada and eastern USA, the common musk turtle *Sternotherus odoratus* breathes with its tongue. Tiny papillae or buds all over the tongue extract oxygen from the water passing over them, enabling this freshwater turtle to remain submerged for many months.

The giraffe *Giraffa camelopardalis* has a long tongue, about 18–20cm (45–50in.) long and, while pink at the base, it is black or purple towards the tip. This is thought to protect the tongue from becoming sunburnt in the searing African sun. It also has large papillae and thick saliva to protect the tongue and the inside of the mouth from the thorny vegetation it eats.

The animal with the longest tongue for its body size is the Ecuadorian tube-lipped nectar bat *Anoura fistulata*. Its tongue extends to 8.5cm (3.4in.), half as long again as the bat's own body. The tongue is anchored near the bat's sternum in its chest, and is used to lick the nectar from flowers. The bat hovers like a hummingbird in front of the long *Centropogon* flower and its tongue probes deep down into the nectar chamber at the bottom. It maintains its position not only by flapping its wings at an extraordinary speed – fifteen times per second – but also by using the same flying technique as an insect. During the wing's downward stroke, a vortex forms along its leading edge, and this swirls around the wing on the upward stroke. It lowers the pressure above the wing, creating lift. The effect is enhanced further because the bat has flexible wing membranes, so it can change the shape of its wings as it flies.

EVOLVING TOGETHER

Morgan's sphinx moth *Xanthopan morgani*, a large tropical species of hawkmoth, has a proboscis that unfurls to a length of more than 25cm (10in.) long, one of the longest of any known insect. It evolved this extraordinary mouthpart to drink the nectar from an equally remarkable flower, one that caught the eye of none other than Charles Darwin. Amongst a batch of dried flowers sent to Darwin from Madagascar was the Christmas star orchid *Angraecum sesquipedale*, which has an exceptionally deep spur, up to 35cm (14in.) long. As many flowers have close associations with pollinating insects, he surmised in a publication dated 1862 that there must be an as yet undiscovered moth with an exceptionally long proboscis that visits this flower in order to drink its nectar. His contemporary Alfred Russel Wallace, co-proponent

21

of the theory of evolution, agreed, having measured the long proboscises of sphinx moths from South America and Africa. Forty-one years later, Walter Rothschild and Karl Jordan found the insect in a Madagascan forest. It was Morgan's sphinx moth, and it operates in a very deliberate way. The moth first hovers in front of a star orchid to check its scent; it backs up 30cm (12in.) or so, and unrolls its long proboscis. It then flies forward, pushing it into the flower's long spur. In this way it can reach the pool of nectar at its base. When it leaves, it carries the star orchid's pollen to the next plant. Flower and insect have co-evolved, each dependent on the other.

A related species of star orchid *Angraecum cadetii,* which grows on trees on the Indian Ocean island of Réunion, does not have the benefit of sphinx moths for pollination, for there are none on the island. Instead, an unknown species of rasping cricket *Glomeremus* pollinates the greenish-white flower. Crickets and grasshoppers usually consume flowers, so this was the first example of a cricket pollinator. The plant, which is thought to have originated on Madagascar, has evolved a shorter nectar tube to accommodate insects other than moths, and its entrance has an uncannily close fit with the head of the cricket. Two other species of star orchid on the island – *A. bracteosum* and *A. striatum* – are pollinated by two small songbirds – the Réunion grey white-eye *Zosterops borbonicus* and the Réunion white-eye *Z. olivaceus*.

FEEDING TIME

Horned lizards *Phrynosoma*, which live in the arid lands of south-west North America, feast on harvester ants *Pogonomyrmex*. These ants have formidable biting jaws and a venomous sting, yet the lizards eat them with impunity – and they have a neat trick that enables them to do so. The lizard stands beside an ant trail and picks off the ants with its tongue. The lizard does not chew the ant – as many other lizards would do – instead each ant is sent immediately to the back of the throat where a shag-carpet-like collection of mucus-secreting cells coat it with a gob of mucus. This wraps up the ant so it can't do any damage inside the lizard. It also acts as a lubricant so the prey can be swallowed rapidly. While many ant-eating animals, such as anteaters and aardvarks, have mucus on their tongues for licking up ants, this is the first known example of incapacitating ants with balls of mucus.

Constricting snakes, such as the boas *Boa constrictor,* stop squeezing their prey when its heart stops. Constriction requires seven times more energy than when at rest so by monitoring the prey in this way the snake can save its strength for eating.

Nile crocodiles *Crocodylus niloticus* in East African rivers, such as the Mara River, have a lean time for most of the year, making do with a few fish, but come the great wildebeest migration, when thousands of animals must cross to reach pastures new, there's a sudden glut of food. In order to take best advantage of it, the crocs must be able to quickly digest large quantities of meat and bones. They do this by pumping carbon dioxide-rich, deoxygenated blood via the left aorta, directly to the stomach. Crocodiles have a four-chambered heart, like we do, but they can revert to a more primitive system when it suits them. Normally deoxygenated blood goes to the lungs via the pulmonary artery, but when a crocodile has eaten a large meal it can be diverted to the stomach where gastric glands use the carbon dioxide to boost the production of gastric acid. It's so effective that crocodiles produce ten times more gastric acid than has been recorded in any other animal, perfect for digesting a large, bony meal like a haunch of wildebeest.

All species of octopuses are venomous. While the blue-ringed octopus *Hapalochlaena* is exceptionally dangerous to humans, other species reserve their venom for predation, such as paralysing the muscles of clams in order to open their shells.

The deep-sea Dana octopus squid *Taningia danae* is found at depths of 240–940m (790–3,085ft) in tropical and sub-tropical waters. It can grow to more than 2.3m (7.6ft) long, and was once thought to be a sluggish creature. Japanese scientists, working off Chichi-jima in the North Pacific, know differently. They obtained video of the squid in its natural environment and found it to be very aggressive. They also saw that it is able to swim fast – up to 2.5m (8ft) per second, both forwards and backwards, by flapping its large and muscular fins, and change direction rapidly by bending its body – but they weren't expecting its attack behaviour. As it approaches prey, the squid spreads its arms and emits blinding flashes of light from photophores along the underside of its arms. It is thought the pulses of light disorientate the prey at the critical moment the squid makes a grab. It might also illuminate the target so the squid can better judge its distance, and young squid have been seen trying to intimidate predators by swimming at them with arms flashing. Away from the killing fields, the flashes might also be used in courtship.

Australia's koala *Phascolarctos cinereus* must be the fussiest eater of all marsupials. It eats almost exclusively the leaves of eucalyptus trees, and it is very selective about which species and even which individual trees it visits. Key to its decision is the size of the tree and its neighbours and the taste of the leaves. A tree is deemed attractive if it is large and surrounded by smaller unpalatable trees, but large palatable trees surrounded by more large palatable trees can be attractive, too. As for taste, koalas tend to avoid leaves containing high levels of toxic chemicals known as formylated phloroglucinol compounds (FPCs).

Proboscis monkeys *Nasalis larvatus* in Malaysia chew the cud like cows. They regurgitate food – mostly leaves – and then re-chew it and swallow it again.

The mole (Family: Talpidae) appears to have six digits on its front feet, but its extra thumb is actually a modified sesamoid wrist bone. It effectively widens the foot, making it good for digging tunnels and chasing after worms. The only other mammal known to have a sixth digit is the giant panda *Ailuropoda melanoleuca*. Its extra thumb is also a modified sesamoid wrist bone, which helps the panda hold the bamboo on which it feeds.

The tayra *Eira barbara* – a 60cm (2ft) long, tree-climbing member of the weasel family with a 45cm (18in.) long bushy tail – plans for the future. Just as we put unripe avocados and bananas aside to ripen, the tayra will collect unripe green plantains, which are inedible, and hide them away until they ripen and the pulp is soft. They hide them in plantations rather than the forest, which scientists from the University of Costa Rica discovered was the safest place to keep them from prying eyes. Caching as such is not unusual. Squirrels hide nuts and shrews stash extra insects – leftovers for a rainy day – but the tayra is different: it seems to be thinking about its hunger a few days in the future and planning for it. It's thinking ahead, something that's shown by one other animal – us.

BIRD FEEDERS

The red-necked phalarope *Phalaropus lobatus*, a shorebird found in the northern hemisphere, exploits the physical properties of water to defy gravity when feeding on plankton. Its bill is the wrong shape for sucking things up, so it has evolved an alternative system. It pecks at the water, taking in small droplets, and then opens and closes its bill rapidly. Surface tension does the rest. The droplets move 'uphill', taking the food with them towards the mouth.

European great tits *Parus major* may be small song-birds but they can be fiendish predators. In winter they do the most astonishing thing – they enter caves and feed on hibernating pipistrelle bats *Pipistrellus pipistrellus*. The birds live in north-east Hungary, where the winters are especially hard, and the bats live in caves with large entrances. Light penetrates into the nearest chambers and the birds can navigate in the semi-darkness. They home in on the sounds bats make when they're disturbed, and the birds are in and out of the cave with their prey in their bills within fifteen minutes.

Western scrub jays *Aphelocoma californica* get very stressed ... at least, that's the conclusion of one researcher at the University of Groningen. These birds hide food, like most crow-like birds, but if they believe other birds are watching they re-cache the food, time and again until they are on their own, and then re-cache it one more time, just to be sure. It was thought that the birds were being clever, but a new computer program suggests that they're actually stressed. Unfortunately, all this moving about means that a bird forgets where it stored everything and becomes even more stressed! Researchers are now trying to test in the wild whether the birds really are stressed or smart.

Hummingbird (Family: Trochilidae) bills are designed to sip nectar from flowers, but the birds themselves cannot live on this sugary solution alone. They need proteins, fats and other dietary essentials so they have to catch small insects, too; in fact, a hummingbird needs the equivalent of 300 fruit flies a day just to keep going. Catching so much food must be quite a challenge, but the hummingbird's bill has another design feature that helps the bird catch its prey. Most insect-eating birds have a cartilage hinge at the base of the bill but in the hummingbird the entire bill is solid bone. Using high-speed video, researchers at the University of Connecticut discovered that the lower bill is also thin and flexible like a diving board, and when the bill is opened it can flex back as much as 25 per cent. This downward bending puts stress on the bone, storing elastic energy. When the bill is closed, all this energy is released and it snaps shut in less than a hundredth of second. With such an effective trap, the hummingbird can grab insects in midair with consummate ease.

WORLD'S LARGEST BIRDS

The world's largest living bird is Africa's ostrich *Struthio camelus*. An adult male reaches a height of 2.8m (9ft). The eggs laid by female ostriches are the largest eggs in the world. Each one can weigh 1.4kg (3.09lb), over twenty times the size of a chicken's egg and enough for an omelette to feed ten people.

The bird with the longest wingspan is the wandering albatross *Diomedea exulans*, with a wingspan of 3.65m (12ft). The birds fly great distances, rarely flapping their wings; instead, they use the updraught at the leading edge of waves to stay aloft.

The world's largest flying bird is the Andean condor *Vultur gryphus*, with a wingspan of 3.2m (10.5ft) and a weight of 15kg (33lb), while the heaviest birds capable of flight are male Eurasian great bustards *Otis tarda* and African kori bustards *Ardeotis kori*, both weighing in at 16kg (35lb).

Several birds of prey vie for the title 'biggest eagle'. The Philippine eagle *Pithecophaga jefferyi* is generally considered the longest. Steller's sea eagle *Haliaeetus pelagicus* is the heaviest, and South America's harpy eagle *Harpia harpyja* the most powerful. Australia's wedge-tail eagle *Aquila audax* has the greatest wingspan at 2.83m (9.29ft), with the Himalayan golden eagle *Aquila chrysaetos daphanea* coming a close second at 2.77m (9.09ft).

The largest living penguin is the emperor penguin *Aptenodytes forsteri*, which grows up to 1.35m (4.43ft) tall, but about 40 million years ago there was a penguin *Anthropornis nordenskjoeldi* that stood 1.7m tall (5.58ft), almost as tall as an average man.

Two species – the Eurasian eagle owl *Bubo bubo* and Blakiston's fish owl *Bubo blakistoni* – share the title of 'biggest owl'. They can be 0.75m tall (2.5ft). Blakiston's is found on the coast of Russia's Far East and also in Japan, where it feeds on fish and amphibians, as well as small mammals. The great grey owl *Strix nebulosa* from the boreal forests has the greatest wingspan, up to 0.83m (2.72ft).

The world's largest parrot is the hyacinth macaw *Anodorhynchus hyacinthinus* of South America. It can be up to 1.2m (3.94ft) long, from the top of its head to the tip of its long tail, and have a wingspan of 1.4m (4.6ft). The flightless kakapo *Strigops habroptila* from New Zealand is heavier, up to 3.5kg (7.7lb).

The largest game bird is North America's wild turkey *Meleagris gallopavo*, with a record 16.85kg (37lb) in weight and a length of 1.44m (4.72ft) confirmed for a specimen shot in 2002.

The largest swan is North America's trumpeter swan *Cygnus buccinator*. It is up to 1.82m (6ft) long, and has a wingspan of 3m (9.8ft). The heaviest was a mute swan *Cygnus olor*, which lived in Poland and weighed 23kg (51lb). It was so heavy it couldn't take off.

GIANT REPTILES AND AMPHIBIANS

The biggest crocodile and the world's largest living reptile is the saltwater crocodile *Crocodylus porosus* of Australia and Southern Asia. The largest specimens are over 6m (20ft) long and weigh over 1,360kg (2,998lb), but in historic times even larger animals have been reported – up to 9m (30ft) long. Today, the largest living crocodile is thought to be a 7m (23ft) male in Bhitarkanika National Park on the Orissa coast of India, the location also of several white crocodiles. 'Salties', as they're known in Australia, are extremely dangerous to people, killing an average of two people a year in northern Australia.

The largest lizard is the Komodo dragon *Varanus komodoensis* of Indonesia. The largest reliably measured dragon was a captive one and was 3.1m (10.17ft) long and weighed 165.5kg (365lb).

The longest lizard, however, is Salvadori's monitor or 'tree-crocodile' *Varanus salvadorii* of Papua New Guinea, with males claimed to be 4.6m (15ft) long. Unlike the bulky Komodo dragon, much of its length is in its slender tail.

Generally, a healthy dose of scepticism is needed when it comes to reptile size and none more so than with giant snakes. Exaggeration is rife. The green anaconda *Eunectus murinus* of South America is generally regarded as the world's heaviest with specimens in excess of 227kg (500lb) and the longest is Asia's reticulated python *Python reticulatus* with lengths close to 10m (33ft). In both cases much bigger animals have been claimed but not verified.

The titles 'world's largest living amphibian' and the 'world's biggest salamander' are shared by two species – the Chinese giant salamander *Andrias davidianus*, which can reach a length of 1.83m (6ft), and the Japanese giant salamander *Andrias japonicus*, which has a maximum length of 1.53m (5ft), although greater lengths have been claimed. Both are endangered species and the Chinese species is critically endangered.

The world's largest frog is Africa's goliath frog *Conraua goliath*. It can weigh up to 3.8kg (8.4lb) and its body measures almost 40cm (16in.) from its snout to its vent. It generally eats worms and large insects, such as dragonflies, but is quite capable of taking small snakes and baby crocodiles. The crocodiles get their own back later in life when they eat the frogs. It lives only in Cameroon and Equatorial Guinea and is rated by the International Union for the Conservation of Nature (IUCN) as endangered.

The world's largest toad is the cane toad *Bufo marinus*, native to South and Central America. It was introduced to Australia to control the cane beetle *Dermolepida albohirtum*, a pest of sugar cane, and became a pest itself. It can grow to 33cm (13in.) long, and produces a milky and highly toxic secretion in glands behind the ears. The toxins affect the heart of any animals unwise enough to grab and eat this species. However, the Australian meat ant *Iridomyrmex purpureus* appears to be immune to the poison and attacks young toads. Native frogs and toads naturally avoid meat ants, but the introduced cane toad doesn't move and youngsters are eaten alive.

MIGHTY BITE

The animal with the world's most powerful and reliably measured bite is a 4.59m (15ft) saltwater crocodile *Crocodylus porosus* with a bite force of 16,414 Newtons (N). Compare this with human jaws closing with a bite force of just 890N! It's thought that bigger salties are likely to have even more powerful jaws. The bite strength of a 6.7m (22ft) long animal has been estimated to be 27,531–34,250N, and the extinct monster crocodile *Deinosuchus,* which grew to 11m (36ft) long and lived 75 million years ago, would have had the staggering bite force of 102,803N, significantly more than the value for the jaws of the extinct dinosaur *Tyrannosaurus rex,* which would have been about 57,000N. Researchers at Florida State University, who reported on the crocodiles in March 2012 after measuring captive animals, found in an earlier 2005 study a wild 4m (13ft) long American alligator *Alligator mississippiensis* had a bite of 13,255N, putting it into second place. The strength in crocodile jaws, however, is only evident when the animal closes them. The muscles that open its jaws are very weak, and so the jaws are easily held shut, even by human hands.

Bite-forces for other crocodilians in the Florida State University study include:

Length m (ft)		Bite-force (N)
3.32 (10.9)	Mugger crocodile *C. palustris*	7,295
4.05 (13.3)	false gharial *Tomistoma schlegelii*	6,450
3.40 (11.2)	Orinoco crocodile *C. intermedius*	6,276

3.15 (10.3)	New Guinea crocodile *C. no-vaeguineae*	5,938
2.63 (8.6)	Siamese crocodile *C. siamensis*	4,577
2.84 (9.3)	Morelet's crocodile *C. more-letii*	4,399
3.18 (10.4)	American crocodile *C. acutus*	4,355
3.04 (10)	black caiman *Melanosuchus niger*	4,310
2.61 (8.6)	Nile crocodile *C. niloticus*	3,172
2.46 (8)	Cuban crocodile *C. rhombifer*	3,127
2.44 (8)	Mindoro crocodile *C. mindo-rensis*	2,736
1.83 (6)	W African dwarf croc *Oste-olaemus tetraspis*	2,509
2.62 (8.6)	long-snouted W A croc *Mecis-tops cataphractus*	2,447
1.77 (5.8)	broad-nosed caiman *Caiman latirostris*	2,420
3.34 (11)	gavial or gharial *Gavialis gan-geticus*	2,006
2.15 (7)	Australian freshwater croco-dile *C. johnstoni*	1,836

Source: Erickson et al. (2012) Insights into the Ecology and Evolutionary Success of Crocodilians Revealed through Bite-Force and Tooth Pressure Experimentation.[*]

Another contender for the title of most powerful bite is the great white shark *Carcharadon carcharias*. A 2008 computer model worked out that a

---

[*] PLoS ONE 7 (3): e31781.doi:10.1371/journal.pone.0031781

large 6.4m (21ft) long shark has a bite force of just under 18,216N, but direct measurements have yet to confirm this.

The jaws of the spotted hyena *Crocuta crocuta* have been measured at 4,500N and lions and tigers have a bite force of about 4,450N.

WORLD'S LARGEST LAND MAMMALS

The world's largest animal on land is Africa's savannah elephant *Loxodonta africana*. The largest recorded was a bull shot in 1974 in Angola. It stood 4.17m (13.7ft) at the shoulder. The mounted body of a rogue bull shot in 1955, which stands at 4.01m (13.2ft), is at the Smithsonian National Museum of Natural History in Washington D.C.

The world's largest-living primate is the male eastern lowland gorilla *Gorilla beringei graueri*, with a height of 1.94m (6.37ft) and weighing 266kg (587lb). It lives in the rainforest of eastern Democratic Republic of Congo.

The largest monkey is the male mandrill *Mandrillus sphinx* – 1m (3.3ft) tall and 50kg (110lb) in weight, with a bright red and blue face and bottom. It lives in the forests of Cameroon, Gabon, Equatorial Guinea and the Democratic Republic of Congo where large troops or 'hordes' have been seen with up to 845 individuals.

Two types of bear share the laurels for 'largest bear' and 'largest land-living predator' – the polar bear *Ursus maritimus*, sometimes considered a marine mammal, and the Kodiak bear, a subspecies of the brown bear *Ursus arctos middendorffi*. A Kodiak bear can be 3m (10ft) tall when standing on its hind legs.

The largest living rodent is the capybara *Hydrochoerus hydrochaeris* of South America. Capybaras reach 1.5m (5ft) long and stand 0.9m (3ft) at the shoulder. They're often seen in the shallows of tropical South American rivers and oxbows.

The largest marsupial is the male red kangaroo *Macropus rufus* of Australia. It can stand 2.18m (7ft) tall. Rogue males can be very aggressive, causing serious injury to people. The most celebrated case was in 2011, when a large male red kangaroo attacked and nearly killed a 94-year-old woman while she was putting out her washing in her garden in Charleville, Queensland.

The largest bat is the giant golden-crowned flying fox *Acerodon jubatus* from the Philippines. It has a wingspan of 1.8m (6ft) and weighs 1.5kg (3.3lb). The lighter large flying fox *Pteropus vampyrus* can have a greater wingspan of up to 2m (6.6ft)

The largest big cat is the Siberian tiger *Panthera tigris altaica*, which can be 3.5m (11.5ft) long and weigh up to 310 kg (683lb), depending on what it's just eaten.

The tallest animal on the planet is Africa's giraffe *Giraffa camelopardalis*, with a height of 5.8m (19ft).

The largest deer is the moose *Alces alces*, standing 2.4m (8ft) at the shoulder. It lives in the forests of the northern hemisphere of both the Old and New World.

The largest wild pig is the giant forest hog *Hylochoerus meinertzhageni* from the African rainforests. It can be 2.55m (8.4ft) long.

WHALE OF AN APPETITE

Blue whales *Balaenoptera musculus* plough through the water and dive down to 500m (1,640ft), before making a U-turn to the surface while opening their gigantic maw to gulp in krill filtered from the water. It's a gargantuan effort from an enormous animal feasting on very small prey, but it's worth it. The whale obtains a hundred times more energy from its food than it expends collecting it.

The fin whale *Balaenoptera physalus* motors through the water at even greater speeds. When feeding it dives down to 180m (600ft) in search of huge swarms of krill, its forward motion brought abruptly to a halt when it opens its mouth. The lower jaw drops and the throat pleats unfold, like a parachute, and in just three seconds the mouth engulfs 60,500 litres (18,000 gallons) of seawater and krill. The mouth shuts in the next three seconds, the tongue squeezing out water through the baleen plates, and the whale swallows the trapped krill. This bus-sized mouthful of water generally yields about 9kg (20lb) of krill, but the whale can feed like this every thirty seconds, so in about four hours it can acquire enough food to keep itself going for the entire day.

Grey whales *Eschrichtius robustus* feeding in Puget Sound in the Pacific Northwest are inadvertently feeding the ducks. The whales scour the seabed for ghost shrimps (Family: Thalassinidea) and other invertebrates, and as they progress along the seafloor they leave great pits and clouds of sediment chock-full of seafood in their wakes. And, where nature creates a feeding opportunity, there's sure to be something that takes advantage of it, in this case sea ducks. Surf scoters *Melanitta perspicillata* and white-winged scoters *M. deglandi* have been seen to follow the whales, sometimes feeding right alongside them, picking off the sea creatures that have been disturbed as the whales plough up the seabed.

In a cove on Unimak Island, the largest and easternmost of the Aleutian Islands, about 160 killer whales *Orcinus orca* intercept and kill grey whale calves and yearlings. The calves and their mothers, heading north through Isanotski Strait, between the island and the Alaskan Peninsula, migrate from their breeding grounds at Baja California to their breeding grounds in the Bering Sea, and for some the strait is a death trap. The orcas ambush and cull up to 300 calves during the course of a season. They grab pectoral fins and pull calves below to drown them or they tear out the throat and grab at the tongue so they die of blood loss. If they can, they drive them into water about 20–30m (65–100ft) deep, but if the prey swims into very shallow water, a mother and calf are more likely to survive for the orcas won't follow. They also abandon attacks on calves with aggressive mothers, searching elsewhere for easier prey. They also avoid driving the whales into waters deeper than 300m (985ft) for any carcass will sink into the depths, out of reach. Selecting the safety of the mid-ground, the orcas leave the carcasses on the seabed and come back to gorge on them for several days following the initial hunt, the first example of caching in a killer whale population. The sunken whales also attract other animals. Pacific sleeper sharks *Somniosus pacificus* come up from the depths and eat their fill, and, along the shore, an orca kill is like a dinner bell to waiting grizzly bears *Ursus arctos horribilis*, red foxes *Vulpes vulpes* and bald eagles *Haliaeetus leucocephalus*. They scavenge on anything that's washed ashore and, should an entire carcass float into the shallows, up to nineteen bears might be feeding on or around it at any one time.

Off the coast of British Columbia, three types of killer whale are known: resident pods, which eat salmon and other fish; transient pods, which specialises in marine mammals; and offshore pods whose food until now has been a mystery. In 2008, researchers from the Pacific Biological Station in Nanaimo witnessed orcas feasting on a Pacific sleeper shark and the team found a piece of its liver to prove it. Since then offshore pods have been seen attacking blue sharks *Prionace glauca*, as well as more feeding incidents with sleeper sharks, including a pod tackling seven sharks in three hours in Prince William Sound. The bigger the shark, the bigger the liver, so the orcas target the sharks with the biggest livers, a delicacy it seems for offshore orcas, but there is a drawback: the sharks' rough skin wears down the orcas' teeth.

It has long been thought that whales and dolphins have lost their sense of smell, but American and Japanese researchers have discovered that the bowhead whale *Balaena mysticetus* hasn't. While dissecting the brain of a whale caught in a subsistence hunt by local people on the north coast of Alaska, they found olfactory nerves that in other mammals normally connect the brain to the nose. At the end of these they discovered intact olfactory hardware. They also found DNA coding for olfactory receptor proteins, which are associated with the sense of smell, and an olfactory bulb in the brain that, size for size, is the equivalent of the bulb of a macaque or baboon, both creatures with a good sense of smell. Speculation is that although bowheads can't smell underwater, they can smell their prey from airborne smells. Krill, for example, smell like boiled cabbage, something not lost on the seabirds and seals that prey on them, and the bowhead is a krill specialist. In addition, the blowhole of a bowhead has two separate openings so the whale might get directional cues too. The Inupiat people have long known that bowheads have a sense of smell, for they noticed that bowheads went further offshore when they lit fires. Science is just catching up.

Humpback whales *Megaptera novaeangliae* have a broad repertoire of techniques to feed on small fish and krill. They might lunge across the surface, sometimes with several whales moving together in an echelon formation, and they might stun prey with their flukes or flippers, but the most ingenious is 'bubble-netting', when several whales work together. Some of the whales dive below a shoal of fish and blow bubbles from their blowholes as they spiral slowly upwards to form a shrinking column of bubbles, effectively a 'net' that encloses and concentrates the shoal. Other whales dive deeper and herd the fish upwards, some of them emitting piercing screams to frighten the fish. Finally, all the whales swim up inside the net with mouths agape and take mouthfuls of seawater and fish, breaking through the surface like a gigantic and untidy flower. The water is drained away through the whales' baleen plates and the fish swallowed. Then, they do it all over again. Whales that cooperate like these tend to stick together, not only for the feeding season, but also for several years. They go their separate ways to the breeding grounds but when they return again, they pick up where they left off – but it is only the females that work together, not males.

At night, humpback whales on and around the Stellwagen Bank, between Cape Cod and Cape Ann on the east coast of the USA, make sounds known as 'megapclicks'. They consist of trains of clicks and buzzes reminiscent of the echolocation signals used by dolphins and toothed whales. Until this discovery, reported in 2007 by researchers from several US marine institutes, baleen whales were not known to make these sounds. They only make the sounds at night, and instruments attached to their bodies record that at the end of the click train they roll their bodies sharply, indicative of feeding. Whether the whales are echolocating to feed at night is not yet known, but it certainly sounds as if they are.

Humpback whales are not averse to stealing the food of others. They'll jump into someone else's bubble-net and steal fish, for example, but in south-east Alaska they steal from seabirds. Flocks of murres *Uria* round up shoals of herring *Clupea*, chasing them into tight bait-balls from which they pluck out individual fish. Gulls drop in to pick them off the surface. The humpbacks, however, wait until the birds have done all the work, then one will rush up from below and scoop up the ball of fish in one enormous gulp.

Northern right whales *Eubalaena glacialis* in the Gulf of Maine feed on the algae-grazing copepod *Calanus finmarchicus*, and the behaviour of the tiny crustacean influences the behaviour of the whale. The copepods undertake a daily vertical migration, descending to depths by day to avoid herring *Clupea harengus* and sand lance *Ammodytes dubius*, return-ing to the surface to graze on phytoplankton at night. The whales follow the copepods down, for they can feed at depths of 180m (600ft), and then back to the surface to feed at night, but here they're in danger. While they feed in the dark, they're more liable to be hit by ships and for a critically endangered popula-tion, every whale counts.

SEAFOOD CONNOISSEURS

Dolphins are accomplished chefs. A female Indo-Pacific bottlenose dolphin in Spencer Gulf, South Australia, has been seen to prepare a dish of calamari. First, she herded cuttlefish, which had been hiding in seaweed, out into the open and over to a patch of sandy seabed. She then stood on her head and pinned down a cuttlefish with her snout, killing it instantly with a rapid downward thrust accompanied by a loud click, smashing the cuttlebone. Lifting the broken body, she hit it several times with her snout to get rid of the ink. Finally, she scraped the body on the sand to remove the bits of cuttlebone. When all she was left with were the soft parts, she gobbled them down; and she's not the only dolphin chef in Australia. According to researchers at the University of Exeter, other dolphins attending the cuttlefish spawning grounds prepare their meals in the same way. Dolphins have also been seen removing the venomous spines from flathead fish *Platycephalus* and filleting metre-long golden trevally *Gnathanodon speciosus* into manageable chunks.

Common dolphins in the Atlantic Ocean are like gourmets at a fish market. According to marine biologists from the University of Rochelle, they carefully select what fish they eat. While other marine predators, such as most sharks and billfish, eat just about anything that moves, short-beaked common dolphins *Delphinus delphius* in the Bay of Biscay are choosy, preferring energy-rich lanternfish over any other food. They simply ignore any fish containing less than 5kJ per gram of energy, even if they are abundant. Common fish in the vicinity include *Xenodermichthys copei* with 2.2kJ, Bean's sawtooth eel *Serrivomer beanii* with 2.1kJ, and Boa dragonfish *Stomias boa ferox*, but the dolphins don't bother to catch them, preferring two species of much less common lanternfish – Kroyer's lanternfish *Notoscopelus kroeyeri*, which contains 7.9kJ per gram of energy, and the glacier lanternfish *Benthosema glaciale* with 5.9kJ. Other research suggests that striped dolphins *Stenella coeruleoalba* also like lanternfish more than any other.

Some killer whales *Orcinus orca* are picky eaters. The resident killer whales, which live in and around Puget Sound on North America's Pacific coast, eat fish, in particular salmon, but they're fussy about which species. They prefer the large Chinook salmon

Oncorhynchus tshawytscha, even though coho *O. kisutch* and sockeye *O. nerka* salmon are more abundant. The Chinooks have more energy-rich fat, but how does a killer whale know the difference? University of Washington and Hawaii bioacousticians believe they know how. The Chinook salmon has a significantly smaller swim bladder, about half the size of the other two species, and it's this that reflects the killer whales' echolocation sounds. By reading the returning signals that bounce off the salmon, a whale can identify a Chinook at 100m (330ft) or more.

In the Antarctic, killer whales are equally fussy about what they eat. There are three types: type A, which specialise in catching minke whales *Balaenoptera acutorostrata*; type B, which will take the occasional whale, but prefer seals; and type C, which seem to dine almost exclusively on Antarctic toothfish *Dissostichus mawsoni*. The seal-eaters are even harder to please: they prefer Weddell seals *Leptonychotes weddellii*, even though other species, such as crabeater seals *Lobodon carcinophagus*, are more numerous. They catch their prey by swimming in line abreast directly at an ice floe on which a seal is resting. The wave, which these pack-ice killers create, swamps or capsizes the slab of ice, throwing the seal into the water, where it is harassed until it is exhausted. It's then carefully skinned and dismembered before being shared by all the members of the pod. The whale-killers also deviate from their normal fare. They sometimes take penguins, which they carefully pluck and skin, and then eat the breast meat, leaving the rest.

In New Zealand's Whangarei Harbour orcas catch eagle rays *Myliobatis tenuicaudatus*, but they're finicky about what part they eat. They consume only the oil-rich liver and leave the rest. And they sometimes play with their food. They dig the rays out of the seabed and bring them to the surface where they toss them about like frisbees. Similarly, off the Patagonian coast of South America, orcas play with their food like a cat playing with a mouse. The orcas come right into very shallow water and pluck juvenile sea lions *Otaria flavescens* and elephant seals *Mirounga leonina* right off the beach and drag them out to deeper water. Then, using their powerful tails, they bat their unfortunate victims high into the air, time and again.

In the murky North Sea, common or harbour seals *Phoca vitulina* can find food by using their whiskers. The whiskers detect disturbances in the water left in a fish's wake, and they are remarkably sensitive. In laboratory tests by biologists from the University of Rostock, a captive seal was able to distinguish the different wakes made by paddles of different shapes and sizes. This means that seals in the wild have the capability to tell which fish are worth chasing, e.g. whether they are big or small, meaty or scrawny, simply by examining the wake they leave behind.

DOLPHINS AND FISHERMEN

Between Mandalay and Kyaukmyaung on the upper reaches of the Ayeyawady River (formerly the Irrawaddy River) in Myanmar is a 72km (45 miles) long stretch where local cast-net fishermen and Irrawaddy dolphins *Orcaella brevirostris* cooperate to catch fish. The fishermen communicate with the dolphins by banging a conical wooden pin on the side of their canoes, slapping the water with a paddle, jiggling the lead weights that fringe the bottom of the cast-net or making guttural sounds. The dolphins respond by spyhopping and swimming excitedly. When a dolphin signals by raising and splashing its tail fluke, which probably frightens the fish towards the waiting fishermen, they throw their nets and haul in the catch. The dolphins collect up any fish that are stunned or chase any darting away from the net. Calves wait nearby with a babysitter, while the rest of the dolphins join in the fishing, but if a babysitter isn't available the mother waits with her calf and misses out on the hunt.

On the Tapajos River in Brazil local fishermen call up the Amazon river dolphin *Inia geoffrensis* by tapping the sides of their canoes and whistling. The dolphins appear, herding the fish towards the boat, where the fishermen spear them.

At Laguna, in southern Brazil, wild bottlenose dolphins *Tursiops truncatus* and fishermen cooperate to catch mullet at the entrance to a series of interconnecting brackish water lagoons. The lagoon nearest the sea is Lagoa Santo Antonio, and here local fishermen follow a ritual involving just one pod of dolphins and no others, which started in 1847. The men wade into the sea carrying a cast-net and stand in line along the shore. The water is murky so they rely on the dolphins to known when to throw their nets. The dolphins first appear some distance away, and then swim towards the line of men. One by one they submerge and swim closer. Suddenly one will break the surface directly in front of the fishermen and turn on its side. This is the signal to cast the nets.

If the dolphin fails to roll, the fishermen will not cast; in fact, the dolphins seem to dictate the entire hunt, determining where the men should stand and when they should make a move. The dolphins' reward is 10–12kg (22–27lb) of mullet a day. It's thought that these particular dolphins continue to cooperate in this way because mothers in the pod teach their offspring how to herd the mullet. Mothers gently nudge their youngsters towards the shoals and they pick up the herding technique by example.

In the Bay of Timiris in the Banc d'Arguin National Park, Mauritania, the local people – the *Imraguen*, meaning 'gatherers of life' – catch fish with the help of the common bottlenose dolphins and Atlantic humpbacked dolphins *Sousa teuszii*. The fishermen anticipate the arrival of the fish in September, when the mullet head south. Children splash the water to summon the dolphins, and then they watch and wait. The first sign is a line of dorsal fins, and sometimes the pod can be a hundred strong. They swim about 25m (80ft) out and parallel to the shore, driving the mullet ahead of them. The fishermen rush into the water with their hand-woven nets and block the path of the fish, and as one shoal is surrounded another net is laid further out from the first, and so on throughout the day. The fish jump in all

directions, surrounding the fishermen with flashes
of silver and showering them with shiny scales. In
the confusion, the dolphins avoid the nets and weave
in and out of the fishermen's legs, taking their share
of the catch.

PECULIAR FOODS

A deep-sea squat lobster *Munidopsis andamanica*
hauled up from 915m (3,000ft) deep has been found
to be eating trees, an unlikely food for a deep-sea
animal until it's realised that waterlogged trunks
and branches eventually sink to the floor of the deep
sea. The squat lobster has bacteria and fungi living
in its gut that provide the enzymes to break down
the cellulose in wood, so it can live off this surprising source of food. 'Wood-falls', as they're known,
provide sustenance for all manner of deep-sea
creatures from wood-boring bivalve molluscs and
marine worms to amphipod crustaceans, shrimps
and other species of crabs.

Bone worms *Osedax* eat the bones of dead whales
that have sunk 3,000m (900ft) to settle on the deep-
sea floor – but they go about it in the most grotesque
way. They start out, like all marine worms, as larvae

that either drift about in the deep-sea plankton or on the mouthparts of crustaceans that eat the whale meat; nobody is sure which. When they find a dead animal they follow chemical clues that lead them to the bones, whereupon they start to change. They develop red, pink, striped or green feathery plumes at one end that act as gills. At the other end, root-like structures grow into the bone and absorb nutrients. They have no gut, but bacteria in the 'roots' are thought to digest proteins and fats in the collagen and cholesterol within the bone. These provide the nutrients that sustain the worm. The visible bone worms are all females. The microscopic males are retained in 'harems' inside a gelatinous tube wrapped around the female's body and release sperm that fertilises the female's eggs. They reproduce rapidly, so whalebones can look as if a shaggy carpet covers them. They also come in waves, like plant succession. First come worms with shallow roots, which are later replaced by worms with deeper roots – and there's even one with a curly pig-like tail that bores into bone debris buried in the mud nearby. Bone worms, or 'bone-eating snot-flowers' as they're known colloquially, were first discovered in 2002 by researchers from the Monterey Bay Aquarium Research Institute. All the different bone worms they have identified so far are entirely new to science and they'll settle on the bones of all sorts of animals that sink to the sea floor, not exclusively whalebones.

Deep-sea fish like spinach! In experiments to see how deep-sea creatures react to a 'plant-fall', scientists from the Royal Netherlands Institute for Sea Research and Aberdeen University sank cages of spinach to a depth of 3,000m (900ft) in the North Atlantic off the coast of Portugal. Almost immediately cusk eels *Spectrunculus* and two species of grenadier fish *Coryphaenoides armatus* and *C. mediterraneus* began to eat the bait, the first time that deep-sea fish have been seen eating plant material. It means these fish, which were thought to be inveterate meat-eaters, are actually generalists, taking advantage of anything that should drop from above. In submarine canyons off the north coast of the Hawaiian island of Moloka'i, huge quantities of kukui nuts supplement the diets of deep-sea animals.

A small Mexican jumping spider *Bagheera kiplingi* has not only an engaging scientific name, but also an odd diet. Most spiders are meat-eaters, but *Bagheera* is mainly a vegetarian, the first known to science. It lives on acacia trees and bushes, where the tree has a symbiotic relationship with stinging *Pseudomyrmex* ants. The ants protect the tree from leaf-eaters and any other creatures that might do it harm, and in return the tree supplies them with hollows in which the ants can nest, along with nectar and tiny food parcels, known as Beltian bodies. The jumping spider is so agile, it avoids the aggressive ants and steals the protein- and fat-rich Beltian bodies from under their noses; in fact, they make up 90 per cent of the spider's diet in Mexico, although the same spiders in Costa Rica eat them 60 per cent of the time, while snacking on nectar, ant larvae and other insects as well. The spiders appear to be onto a good thing, for the ants keep away predators on the lookout for spiders, such as birds.

The bertam palm *Eugeissona* in the Malaysian rainforest smells like a brewery because its nectar is alcoholic. Yeast cells in the flowers ferment their nectar, so that it contains 3.8 per cent alcohol, the highest concentration found in a natural food. Any animal that comes to drink regularly should become inebriated and such a creature is the pen-tailed tree shrew *Ptilocercus lowii*, though it's actually none the worse for having drunk the alcohol-laced nectar. It feeds for up to 138 minutes a night, and analysis of shrew hairs by researchers from the University of Bayreuth revealed that the shrew takes in sixty times the level that is considered excessive drinking in humans. The tree shrews do not behave as if they're drunk, though, and for the moment nobody knows why.

In tests at the University of California, San Francisco, male fruit flies *Drosophila* that failed to mate had low levels of a 'rewards' neurotransmitter or neuropeptide known as NPF, and turned to alcohol-spiked foods as consolation. Flies that mated had high levels of NPF and did not resort to alcohol.

GRUB'S UP!

Generally, parent animals tend to be the providers and their offspring the receivers, but in the North American paper wasp *Polistes dominulus* society there is a surprising role reversal: wasp larvae feed the adults. Items of food, such as caterpillars, are collected by the adult wasps and brought back to the nest, but the adults themselves cannot feed on them; they can only take liquid food. Wasps have a very narrow 'waist' between the thorax and the abdomen where digestion takes place, so chunks of food cannot pass through. Instead, the grub-like wasp larvae, which do not have the constriction, can tackle the food and produce nutrient-rich saliva, some of which can be fed back to the adults. When an adult is hungry, it signals by scraping its abdomen across the nest and receives a ration of food from a larva. The larvae strictly control the amount. They seem to learn just how much to give and if an alien insect should sneak into the nest for a free meal, the larvae reduce significantly the amount delivered if the scraping signal is not given.

The common wasp or yellow jacket *Vespa vulgaris* is found throughout the northern hemisphere, but it was introduced to New Zealand over thirty years ago and is now a serious alien pest. This cunning wasp has found a surprising way of dealing with local competitors, such as ants, for sources of food. It does not waste energy stinging them but instead picks up the ant gingerly and drops it some distance away, before the ant can summon any of its nest mates; the more ants swarming around the food, the farther away is the dropping zone.

Azteca ants in South America live in close association with trumpet trees *Cecropia*. The trees provide the ants with shelter in hollow stems and food in the form of the special nutritive Beltian bodies, while in return the ants defend the tree against leaf-eating animals. However, one species of ant *Azteca andreae*, which lives on *Cecropia obtusa*, ignores the food gifts from the tree and the workers strike out on their own for surprisingly bigger game. The secret of their success is in their feet. The ants line up beneath the edge of the leaf, gripping the velvet-like under-surface with their hook-like feet, in much the same way as velcro. If prey should alight on their leaf, they all rush out and capture it, pulling it down below and out of harm's way. With this system they can hold on to prey thousands of times heavier than they are; in fact, one group was seen to capture and retain a locust weighing 18.61g (0.66oz) – 13,350 times the weight of a single ant.

The common stingless ant *Pachycondyla chinensis*, an invasive species in the USA, has a simple but surprising way to deal with overly large items that need to be taken back to the nest. Having encountered the object, it races back to the nest and grabs another ant in its jaws and carries it to the food. During its transport, the second ant is totally impassive, but when they reach their destination they both set about dismantling the large food item, slicing it up into manageable chunks and carrying them back to the nest.

INSECT FARMERS

Leafcutter ants *Atta* and *Acromyrmex* are arable farmers. They collect leaves from the forest, bring them back to the nest and grow 'fungus gardens'. The fungus breaks down the leaves and the ants feed on the fungus. The crop is kept healthy and disease free with bacteria, which produce a range of antibiotics. The ants also cultivate two more friendly microbes to make proteins. Leaves are rich in sugars but low in nitrogen, so in order to have a balanced diet the ants cultivate two nitrogen-fixing bacteria. The bacteria utilise nitrogen from the air to make ammonia, which is used to manufacture proteins. With other insects that tend fungus gardens, such as termites, the nitrogen fixers are in the gut, but with leafcutter ants, they're actually in the gardens. Over the course of a year, a leafcutter ant colony might convert up to 1.8kg (4lb) of nitrogen from the air, the equivalent of the nitrogen in 10,000sq. metres (12,000sq. yards) of tropical soil. It means trees tend to clump around the ants' nests, snaking their roots into the ants' refuse dumps because they're rich in natural fertiliser.

Several species of common garden ants *Lasius* keep livestock: they herd aphids (Superfamily: Aphidoidea). They bite their wings off to stop them flying away and produce chemicals that stop them growing new ones, and the ants' footprints contain a tranquilising chemical that acts like a fence to contain the aphids in the ant farm. The ants 'milk' the aphids for the honeydew they produce and just occasionally eat the aphids themselves, just like human farmers do with cows, sheep and goats.

Aphids, unlike their ant masters, tend to be untidy. The farm may be littered with the aphids' old, discarded exoskeletons – but there is a reason. Aphids are susceptible to attacks from parasitic wasps and the ants seem unable to protect them, so they leave the old skins around as decoys. The wasps investigate the decoys, so are less likely to attack the living aphids.

Some species of aphids are miniature horticultural-ists and look after their plants. The Japanese aphid *Nipponaphis monzeni* causes its host plant to form a gall and the colony of aphids lives inside. This species has colonies with soldier aphids that not only protect and clean the colony, but also repair the gall. Caterpillars sometimes eat into the gall, rendering the aphid colony susceptible to predators, but the soldiers come to the rescue. They expel their body fluids into the gap, their shrivelled bodies helping to form a scab.

Then the plant itself takes over. It repairs the gall, but it will only do so if it receives the wound-repair signal from the kamikaze soldier aphids.

LIVING TOGETHER

The eastern emerald sea slug *Elysia chlorotica* from the east coast of North America may not look much, but it's an extraordinary creature which behaves partly as an animal and partly as a plant – and it's solar-powered to boot. It's the first animal to be discovered that uses the plant pigment chlorophyll to manufacture its own food. This is the chemical that green plants and plant-like green algae possess to carry out photosynthesis, the process by which carbon dioxide and water are converted into sugars using the Sun's energy. It's the basic level of food production that sustains most of life on Earth. However, the sea slug can carry out this first stage in the food chain itself: it grazes on the green alga *Vaucheria litorea*, rupturing the algal cells, sucks out the cytoplasm and digests it, but retains the chloroplasts. These are the tiny organelles in algal cells that contain the chlorophyll for photosynthesis. Once inside the slug, the chloroplasts keep working, but this requires algal genes to switch them on and off. Remarkably, the sea slug has that covered, too: at some point in the recent past the species sequestered them, so the nucleus in the sea slug's cells contains the genes for plastid function. It passes these genes onto its offspring so they have the ability as well, but they must feed on some algae first to collect chloroplasts before they can start food production. Once it's all up and running, the leaf-shaped sea slugs can survive for the rest of their year-long lives on the food they manufacture themselves – leaves that crawl!

The eggs of North America's spotted salamander *Ambystoma maculatum* turn green. Algae gather around the eggs, feeding on the embryo's waste. The embryos benefit, too, for they gain oxygen from the photosynthesising algae. Researchers have found algae actually *inside* the developing salamanders, the first vertebrate to be found in a symbiotic relationship of this nature. It's similar to the relationship that corals, sea anemones and jellyfish have with zooxanthellae, the single-celled algae-like dinoflagellates that live in their tissues and supply them with extra food.

Feather lice (Phthiraptera: Ischnocera) on birds tend to be the same colour as the host bird's plumage. Sulphur-crested cockatoos *Cacatua galerita* with mainly white plumage, for example, have white lice, while yellow-tailed black cockatoos *Calyptorhynchus funereus* with mainly black plumage have dark lice. It makes them harder to spot when the bird preens with its beak. Lice on the birds' heads, however, are all dark no matter what colour the plumage, probably because the bird scratches its head with its feet and therefore cannot get a look at the bugs, so there's no evolutionary pressure to conform.

A SQUIRT OF WATER

The Pacific lionfish *Pterois volitans* has a unique way of catching smaller fish. As it approaches a target it blows jets of water at it. This overwhelms the prey's lateral line system – part of the fish's sensory system that normally warns it of vibrations in the water – and causes it to face its predator. While it's disorientated, the lionfish grabs it and swallows it headfirst to minimise backward-facing spines getting stuck in its throat.

The archerfish *Toxotes* can shoot down an insect from a branch overhanging the water with a carefully aimed jet of water. It is incredibly accurate, often hitting the target with the first squirt. It achieves this by compensating for the refraction of light at the interface between water and air. When potential prey is spotted, the precise linear relationship between the real elevation of the prey from the nose and the apparent elevation from the eye enables the fish to spit accurately, although accuracy decreases with prey height. Even so, it can hit prey up to 3m above the water by pushing its lips above the surface and spitting. The tongue pushes against a groove in the roof of the mouth, and it can squirt seven or so times in quick succession. It spits at an angle of about 74° from the horizontal, but is able to aim reasonably accurately from 45° to 110°. And, if that fails, the archerfish can always launch itself out of the water and grab an insect from the branch; in fact, the fish prefers this approach. Archerfish tend to gather into shooting parties so squirting jets of water becomes something of a lottery, for the sharpshooter is not necessarily the fish that receives the prize.

Snubfin dolphins *Orcaella heinsohni*, found along the northern coasts of Australia, have an unusual way of catching a meal – they spit at it. They chase fish to the surface and then round them up by shooting jets of water from their mouths. The closely related Irrawaddy dolphin *O. brevirostris* has been seen to do the same thing.

INTEGRATED WEAPONS SYSTEMS

Sharks have a remarkable array of senses to home in on a target, possibly the most diverse of any known predator. Low-frequency sounds travel far underwater so a shark's auditory system is likely to be one of the first senses to detect something interesting from over 1.6km (a mile) away, especially irregularly pulsed broadband sounds that might be made by an injured animal. At a distance of 0.5km (1/3 mile) it can smell blood or body fluids in the water and follow the odour trail upstream to its source. Some sharks can even pick up airborne smells, such as those coming from a whale carcass floating at the surface. At 25m (80ft), in clear water, the shark can see movement, even in dim light, and some have the ability to see colour. Alongside these senses, the lateral line works with the auditory system to give 'touch-at-a-distance', in which the shark can feel the presence of something in the water 100m (330ft) away – but this functions better at two body lengths. And, working with the olfactory sense, the lateral line can detect the trail of odour-tainted disturbances left in the wake of a swimming fish. Guiding the shark for the last few centimetres to its target are electroreceptors in the snout. They detect the electricity associated with muscle activity, such as the prey's beating heart, even if the target is hiding under the sand. These same receptors are also sensitive to temperature, and could be used to detect thermal fronts in the sea where prey might be concentrated. Having taken a bite, the sense of taste determines whether the target is palatable. If it is, then the prey is unlikely to get away.

Sharks are not alone in having the ability to detect electrical activity. Skates and rays and several species of bony fish possess the sense, too. Knifefish (Order: Gymnotiformes) and elephant fish (Family: Mormyridae) actually produce, and receive, weak electric currents. These freshwater fish find their way using electricity and even have electrical conversations. The coelacanth *Latimeria* stands on its head using the rostral organ in its snout to check out electrical signals from prey (the only other fish to have a rostral organ is the anchovy *Engraulis*). North America's paddlefish *Polyodon spathula* is electrically 'tuned' to its zooplankton prey with sensors on its elongated snout.

Some amphibians detect electricity such as the giant salamander *Andrias davidianus*, axolotl *Ambystoma mexicanum* and the cave-dwelling olm *Proteus anguinus*. Australia's platypus and echidna, both egg-laying monotreme mammals, have the sense as well, but it was not expected in a higher placental mammal. Tests with a captive Guiana dolphin *Sotalia guianensis* by workers from Germany's University of Rostock showed that it could detect electrical signals with sense organs in small dark depressions, known as crypts, on its rostrum. This species of dolphin tends to feed on the muddy seabed in murky water, where echolocation at close quarters does not work so well, but an electrical sense that detects activity in the muscles of fish would be just the ticket in this environment.

Since 1956, it has been known that dolphins find their way and locate food by echolocation or biosonar. They produce high-pitched sounds that are focused by the bulbous melon on the forehead and projected as a sound beam into the sea. They then listen for the returning echoes, picking up the sounds on the bottom teeth and transmitting them back to the brain via a fatty channel in the lower jaw. The echoes locate and identify objects in the sea. It was always thought that the dolphin produces a single beam, but work by a young engineering physicist from the University of Lund has revealed that the dolphin actually produces two sound beams simultaneously. They are at different frequencies and can be sent in different directions. It means that the dolphin's echolocation system is probably the most complex of any in the animal kingdom.

BAT ATTACK

Bats' ears are like miniature moving radar dishes; they pick up the echolocation sounds that bounce off objects in the animal's environment, including prey. The ears are flexible, constantly moving and tuned for specific tasks. Bent ears are not so sensitive and sweep around generally for prey, such as moths and other night-flying insects, while also listening out for signs of animals that catch bats, such as owls. Ears held upright and facing directly ahead are more sensitive. They pick up echolocation sounds more effectively and so this configuration is used to gain information about any target being pursued.

Every summer night a life and death battle takes place over our heads as bats try to catch moths and moths try to avoid bats. During these aerial dogfights, some species of moths are able to detect the echolocation sounds made by pursuing bats and take evasive action; after all, bats are shouting their heads off, albeit at ultra-high frequencies which we cannot hear – but the moths can. There is a bat – the rare European barbastelle bat *Barbastella barbastellus* – that is an especially successful moth hunter. At first it was thought that the bat caught earless moths that couldn't hear bats hunting, but research at the University of Bristol revealed that they were catching eared moths with an unexpected hunting strategy: instead of shouting, the barbastella bat whispers. It's a hundred times quieter than most other insect-eating bats, so where other bats are detected up to 30m (100ft) away, this bat can approach to within 3.5m (11.5ft) before the moth knows it's there. By that time, it's too late for the moth to escape. In this way, the barbastella bat can exploit a food source denied to most other bats.

When a bat closes in on a moth, it increases the number of its echolocation calls in order to gain increasingly more accurate information about its fast-moving target. Just before making contact, many bats end their signal with an extremely fast terminal buzz. Researchers were at a loss as to how the bat can make such a sound because mammalian muscles cannot contract so fast, but work at the University of Southern Denmark revealed that a bat's laryngeal (voice box) muscles are 'superfast'. They're capable of contracting up to 200 times per second. Until this work only birds, reptiles and fish have been known to have superfast muscles, so this is the first time they have been found in a mammal.

EYES

The animal with the world's largest eyes is the deep-water colossal squid *Mesonychoteuthis hamiltoni*. An 8m (26ft) long specimen caught in the Ross Sea off the Antarctic coast and examined by researchers in New Zealand had eyes 27cm (11in.) across, bigger than a dinner plate, with a lens as big as an orange and a pupil 9cm (3.5in.) across – and it's thought that even bigger squid exists with even bigger eyes. The squid lives in the ocean depths as deep as 2,000m (6,500ft) – the bathypelagic or 'midnight' zone, where the only light produced is by undersea creatures. It's thought that the colossal squid has massive peepers to see even bigger predators heading towards it, especially the box-car-size sperm whale *Physeter macrocephalus*, the squid's principal enemy. The squid can pick out the whale's outline because as it moves it brushes past tiny deep-sea organisms that glow when disturbed. A big eye means that all these little pinpoints of light are detected from more than 120m (395ft) away, and the squid can take evasive action, using its jet propulsion system to shoot away from danger.

The most complicated eyes must be those of mantis shrimps (Order: Stomatopoda), a group of animals known as 'prawn killers' and 'thumb-splitters' on account of their vicious claws that smash, spear or dismember depending on the shape of their main weapons. Many species are up to 30cm (12in.) long, and some exhibit bright, neon colours on parts of their bodies. Their eyes are compound eyes on mobile stalks, which move independently and constantly. The eye itself consists of two flattened hemispheres packed with tiny eye units, or ommatidia, which are separated by a midband of specialised ommatidia.

The three regions of the eye give the shrimp trinocular vision and excellent depth perception. The midband units can pick up colours from the ultraviolet end of the spectrum through to longer wavelengths (though not infrared), so the shrimp can see in twelve primary colours (compared to humans who can see only in three). It can also perceive different planes of polarised light (a discovery that has implications for future generations of DVDs and CDs). These amazing eyes give the mantis shrimp a clarity underwater denied to other creatures, enabling it to locate and catch prey better than others, especially the transparent creatures it tends to eat. It can also 'talk' to other mantis shrimps through channels of communication invisible to other animals, especially potential predators.

Birds have been described as 'two eyes with wings' because they have the largest eyes relative to their body size. They also see in four primary colours, and birds of prey, such as the common kestrel *Falco tinnunculus*, can see in the near ultraviolet. The urine of many small rodents strongly reflects ultraviolet light and the rodents use their urine to mark their regular foraging trails, like white lines on a road. There is, however, an obvious downside. It exposes the rodents to attacks from the air. The kestrel can see the trail and differentiate between a fresh and a stale trail, so the bird can pinpoint the location of its prey with some degree of certainty. All it needs to do is hover above the trail or a nest entrance and wait for its owner to reappear.

The deep-sea spookfish *Dolichopteryx longipes*, which lives at depths below 1,000m (3,280ft) in the South Pacific, can look up and down at the same time because it has mirrors in its eyes. It's the only vertebrate known to do so. It looks as if it has four eyes but in reality there are only two, each divided into two connecting parts. One part points upwards, giving the fish a view of potential prey above it, and the other points downwards, from where predators might approach. In the darkness, the fish detects the telltale flashes of bioluminescence from other deep-sea creatures, the mirrors in its eyes focusing sharply any light on the sensitive cells of its retina.

One species of deep-sea 'barreleye' fish *Macropinna microstoma* has eyes that can rotate from looking ahead to looking up through its completely transparent, dome-shaped head. It is thought to look for the outline of jellyfish-like siphonophores silhouetted against the faint glow from the surface, and then it swims up slowly to steal the jellyfish's prey.

Sea urchins have eyes in their feet. They have the light-sensitive protein, known as opsin, at the tips and base of their tube feet and, as they have tube feet all over, they can detect light with their entire body, like an enormous compound eye.

Adanson's jumping spider *Hasarius adansoni* judges distances in a novel way and is remarkably accurate when pouncing on prey. Like all spiders, it has eight eyes, two of which are larger than the rest and face forwards. The retina of the two large eyes consists of not one layer of light-sensitive cells, as we have, but four. The spider therefore perceives, say, an image that's in focus on the base layer, but a blurred image on the next layer. The spider judges depth by comparing the two versions of the same scene – one crisp and the other out of focus. In this way, an animal with a miniscule brain can gather and act upon complex visual information. How the jumping spider actually uses the comparison is the next task for the researchers at the Osaka City University.

TELLING THE TIME

Rooks *Corvus frugilegus* breed between February and March so worms are closer to the surface and can be dug out of the soil when their chicks need them, and seed-eaters, such as goldfinches *Carduelis*, breed much later so the seeds they need for their young are readily available. Without a calendar, how do these birds know what time of year it is? The answer is that they detect and appreciate the gradually lengthening days and shortening nights during spring. They do this not with the eyes but with the hypothalamus region of the brain. Here resides a light-sensitive protein known as 'vertebrate ancient opsin' or VA opsin. Light reaches the proteins through the bird's thin skull, providing the bird with its own special calendar.

LOUD VOICES

The African savannah elephant *Loxodonta africana*'s ultra-low-frequency 'rumbles' peak at about 117 decibels, but most of the energy is emitted as infrasounds that people cannot hear. These long-distance, low-frequency calls are given mainly at dawn and dusk, when the air is still and they can be picked up 10km

(6 miles) away. Females rumble to attract solitary bulls from far and wide, and elephants in herds rumble to each other to keep in touch with close relations or to space out groups that might compete for food. Bulls have a 'musth rumble' that dissuades rival bulls from approaching. So well tuned are they to particular frequencies that one bull in Amboseli National Park showed his displeasure by emitting a musth-rumble every time he heard the low frequency sounds produced by the engine of a minibus departing from a lodge 2km (1.2 miles) away.

The loudest landlubber that we humans can hear lives in the forests of South and Central America. The male howler monkey *Alouatta* has a resonating chamber in its throat that amplifies its raucous calls so they carry across the forest for 5–8km (3–5 miles), or sometimes more depending on atmospheric conditions and the density of the trees in the forest. The troop calls mainly in the early morning to warn neighbouring troops to keep away.

Cicadas are loud and relentless, with a unique pair of sound-producing organs called timbals. They're washboard-like plates on either side of the thorax, which are buckled in and out very rapidly by the contraction of powerful and exceptionally fast muscles. The loudest is considered to be the African cicada *Brevisana brevis*, at 106.7 decibels from 50cm (20in.) away. Coming a close second are two large species of North American cicadas *Tibicen walkeri* and *T. resh*, both of which have an alarm call peaking at 105.9 decibels at 50cm (20in.).

Many insects, such as grasshoppers and crickets, make loud sounds by stridulation. Crickets rub their wings together and most grasshoppers rub a leg against their forewing to produce their chirping sounds. Crickets in the family Gryllidae are mostly right-handed, i.e. showing a preference for drawing the right wing over the left. The south Indian tree-cricket *Oecanthus henryi* cannot vibrate its wings so fast in cold weather, so the pitch of its 'song' drops significantly as the temperature plummets. Mole crickets (Family: Gryllotalpidae), with spade-like front feet like a mole, dig tunnels with the shape of a double megaphone to amplify their soft but long-carrying 'churring' songs. The only mammal known to stridulate is the lowland streaked tenrec *Hemicentetes semispinosus* of Madagascar, which rubs its quills together.

The tiny male common coquí frog *Eleutherodactylus coqui* from Puerto Rico is a nocturnal singer that blasts out at 100 decibels from half a metre (20in.) away, making it one of the loudest amphibians in the world. His common name is onomatopoeic for he has two notes to his high-pitched call: a 'ko' part that deters rival males, and a 'kee' part that attracts females. If a male invades another's territory, the two frogs have a 'singing duel'. The first to falter is the loser, the two males having settled the dispute without having come to blows. The species was introduced accidentally to the Hawaiian Islands in the 1980s and now the frog keeps people awake all over the four major islands, gaining it the dubious honour of being placed on a list of the world's 100 worst alien species.

South America's oilbird *Steatornis caripensis* makes an enormous racket. It lives in caves and navigates in and out by a simple form of echolocation. The clicks and squawks, however, are incredibly loud – another 100-decibel belter – and, because they nest and roost in large numbers in a confined space, the noise can be deafening, putting the oilbird amongst the loudest birds in the world.

The male three-wattled bellbird *Procnias tricarunculatus* sings from the treetops. Its chattering song is interspersed with extremely loud 'bongs' that can be 100 decibels and travel more than a kilometre (less than a mile) through the forest.

New Zealand's kakapo *Strigops habroptilus* is a nocturnal ground parrot. The male creates his own amphitheatre – a hollow in the ground that has a 'Hollywood Bowl' effect. It broadcasts his resonating boom up to 5km (3 miles) away, the furthest-carrying song of any bird. The kakapo inflates air sacs in his chest and calls each night for up to four months, making 10,000 or more calls during the breeding season.

Bats seem to be silent hunters, with a just a few faint clicks heard by human ears, but actually the bat is flying along making lots of noise. The sounds are very high frequency or ultrasonic. The greater bulldog bat *Noctilio leporinus* is especially noisy. Its high-frequency screech belts out at 140 decibels – the equivalent of sitting beside an airport runway – and it's adapted to catch fish. However, when big brown bats *Eptesicus fuscus* fly together they remain silent for much of their flight to avoid interfering with each other's echolocation systems.

The Philippine tarsier *Tarsius syrichta* is a nocturnal ET-like primate with huge eyes and, no bigger than the human hand, it is one of the smallest primates. It is often seen at night opening its mouth but emitting no sound, so on a whim researchers from Humboldt State University recorded tarsiers with bat detectors. They were in for a shock: the tarsier, noted for being a 'quiet' animal, is actually highly vocal and chatters away with other tarsiers at very high frequencies – generally about 70 kilohertz but up to 90 kilohertz – well above the human hearing range and that of any other apes or monkeys; in fact, they're chattering away at frequencies double the upper limit of any primate studied to date. It's thought they could benefit in two ways: katydids and moths, which they like to catch and eat, also use very high frequencies, so with the help of their ultrasensitive ears, tarsiers might be able to locate a meal. By pitching their calls way above everything else, they avoid predators eavesdropping on their own channel of communication.

Male lions *Panthera leo* have a large voice box supported by a flexible ligament that creates a large airway enabling them to roar at 114 decibels and be heard 8km (5 miles) away, the loudest roar of any big cat. They roar mainly at night, rarely before 5 o'clock in the evening and not usually after 8 o'clock in the morning.

Grey wolves *Canis lupus* howl at any time of the day or night, often before and after hunts to rally the pack or in response to other packs howling nearby. In the latter case, wolves cheat. They howl together in harmony, together with the echoes and rever-berations of their calls through the forest, so that neighbouring packs find it hard to assess whether there are a few or many wolves in the pack.

Many reptiles emit sounds, such as hissing snakes, rattling rattlesnakes and chirping geckoes, but few make exceptionally loud noises. The exceptions are crocodilians. The American alligator *Alligator mississippiensis*, for example, has no vocal chords, yet it grunts and growls. They can even bellow, a sound that is preceded by a long and loud infrasonic signal – more a vibration than a sound – that causes the surface of the water to 'dance'. The sound is too low for us to hear, but it reaches females some distance away. The bellow itself is also loud, peak-ing at 90 decibels, and once one male starts up others may join in too – a bellowing alligator chorus of up to thirty animals has become known as an 'alligator dance'.

THE (NOT SO) SILENT WORLD

The world's loudest animal is not a great cetacean or pachyderm, but the tiny water boatman *Micronecta scholtzi*, no bigger than a grain of rice. Size for size, it makes the most ruckus of any known animal, a staggering 99.2 decibels, the equivalent of listening to a loud orchestra from the front row of the stalls. It belts out its calls underwater and over 99 per cent of the sound is lost between the water and the air, but they're in the human hearing range and can be heard clearly from a quiet river bank or lakeside. The insect doing the shouting is the male of the species and he makes the sound by rubbing his penis against his abdomen (yes, you read that correctly) in order to attract a mate. The area used for stridulation is no wider than a human hair, so the researchers at the University of Strathclyde and Muséum National d'Historie Naturelle in Paris are at a loss to explain how a tiny insect makes so much noise.

The pistol or snapping shrimp *Alpheus heterochaelis* is another miniature submarine noisemaker that makes an astonishingly loud sound. It's bigger than *Micrinecta*, but still little more than the size of a finger, and it blasts away at 200 decibels. The sound is made by the shrimp's larger claw, which resembles a boxing glove. It's held open until a muscle closes it with lightning speed. However, it's not the pincers snapping together that creates the sound. As the snapper shuts, a tooth-shaped plunger pushes into a niche in the other half of the claw, the impact causing a jet of water to spurt out at high speed, about 100km/h (62mph), leaving a cavitation bubble in its wake. As the bubble collapses, it makes an ear-splitting bang, louder but briefer than a gunshot, and the temperature in the bubble rises instantly to at least 5,000°C (8,540°F). It is accompanied by a flash of light lasting 300 picoseconds (1 picosecond = one trillionth of a second), and researchers at the University of Twente in the Netherlands have dubbed the process 'shrimpoluminescence'. The whole process takes just 300 microseconds, but it's so powerful the shock wave stuns the shrimp's prey – small fish and other shrimp species. It can also use the sound to defend its territory and communicate generally with other pistol shrimps.

In absolute terms, some of the click sounds made by sperm whales *Physeter macrocephalus* are the loudest made by any animal. They can be up to 230 decibels underwater, the equivalent of 170 decibels on land. The clicks consist of pulses of sound that are reflected between air sacs in the whale's nose, so whale biologists are able to work out the size of the nose and therefore the size of the whale to an accuracy of 50cm (1.5ft). They can also work out its age just by listening to the intervals between each pulse. Sperm whales also 'clang', 'chirrup' and 'creak', and emit 'pips', 'squeals' and 'short trumpets'. The whale is thought to use some of these sounds to communicate its identity to others of its kind and the rapid series of clicks often heard at feeding grounds are probably an echolocation system with which to find and identify prey. However, the very loudest clicks might have a more sinister function. The 230-decibel click or 'gunshot' is 10–14 decibels louder than a rifle shot in air just a metre away, and one thought is that this sound could be used as a 'stun gun' to debilitate prey.

Whales are undoubtedly amongst the world's noisiest animals. The world's largest animal, for example, is also one of the world's loudest. The blue whale *Balaenoptera musculus* sings very low frequency songs with such power that they are heard across entire oceans over distances up to 3,000km (6,835 miles). Most of the song is at frequencies too low for humans to hear, but they can be deafening – 188 decibels, louder than a jet engine. Curiously, in recent years, blue whale songs have been dropping in pitch, more than 30 per cent since the 1960s. Nobody knows why.

One curious sound in the ocean, a 20Hz signal, was picked up in the 1960s by military installations listening for enemy submarines. Nobody knew what was emitting it until marine biologists put a microphone array on the sea floor and discovered that fin whales *B. physalus,* the world's second largest animal, were the source of the sound. They belt out low frequency calls at 184–186 decibels, thought to be contact calls between whales in loose herds with individuals scattered over a wide area of ocean. It's their way of keeping in touch.

The most engaging sounds from the sea must be the haunting songs of the bull humpback whale *Megaptera novaeangliae.* They are true songs, like bird songs, with themes and phrases of high and low frequency sounds that are repeated over and again so that a song cycle might last for up to twenty minutes. A bull might sing for the best part of the day and into the night. In the northern hemisphere, where large landmasses separate whale populations, all the males in one population sing the same song – a kind of 'top of the pops' – which evolves during the breeding season. The population takes up a new phrase exceptionally quickly. In the south-east Pacific, for instance, the latest song will always spread from west to east, in a cultural wave from the east coast of Australia to French Polynesia, in little more than a year or two. In a smaller area, it could be as quickly as two to three months, the fastest transmission of a cultural change made by a non-human species. It means that whales in, say, the Atlantic sing very different songs to those in the Pacific.

Fish are surprisingly noisy. Cod *Gadus morhua*, haddock *Melanogrammus aeglefinus* and lythe *Pollachius pollachius* grunt, and the drum and croaker family (Sciaenidae) drum. The oyster toadfish *Opsanus tau* is one of the loudest. Its boat-whistle-like calls have been measured at close to 100 decibels from 60cm (2ft) away. Fish create their sounds with the swim bladder, fin spines, bones or teeth. Triggerfish *Balistes*, for example, gnash their teeth together and seahorses *Hippocampus* rub the back of their skull against a projection on top of the vertebra to make a clicking sound, but the most bizarre method is adopted by the herring: it communicates by breaking wind, producing high-pitched sounds by expelling air from its anus. Researchers from Canada's Bamfield Marine Science Centre called the phenomenon 'Fast Repetitive Tick', which has the mischievous acronym FRT!

SEA MONSTERS

The largest animal that has ever lived on Earth is the blue whale *Baleanoptera musculus*. The biggest known specimen was 33.59m (110ft) long, a female brought ashore in South Georgia in the early 1900s. The blue whale has the largest heart, weighing about 600kg (1,323lb).

The largest fish in the sea is the whale shark *Rhincodon typus*. There have been claims of sharks in excess of 15m (49ft) long, but the largest accurately measured, one caught at Baba Island, Pakistan, was 12.65m (41.5ft) long. It is a filter feeder, gulping down small fish, krill and fish eggs. The second largest is the basking shark *Cetorhinus maximus*, with a maximum length recorded of 12.3m (40.35ft) and a weight of 16 metric tons. It's also a filter feeder.

The largest predatory fish is the great white shark *Carcharodon carcharias*, with accepted lengths up to 7m (23ft), closely followed by the tiger shark *Galeocerdo cuvier*, with similar lengths claimed but not confirmed. Large individuals are capable of slicing a human in two and swallowing each piece whole.

The world's biggest invertebrates are to be found in the deep sea. The longest is thought to be the giant squid *Architeuthus*, which lives in all the world's oceans, but the largest is the colossal squid *Mesonychoteuthis hamiltoni*, from the Southern Ocean around Antarctica. Giant squid are known to be up to 13m long, measured from the caudal fin to the tip of the two long stretchable tentacles, but longer specimens are claimed. In 2007, a US television series expedition in the Sea of Cortez filmed a giant squid said to be 33m (108ft) long, but it was not accurately measured. Giant squid tend to be slender animals, but the colossal squid is a bruiser. At 12–14m (39–46ft) long, it is up there with the giant squid in length, but this creature has a longer, wider and bulkier body and shorter tentacles. Giant squid have suckers with small teeth on the arms and a club at the end of each tentacle, but the colossal squid has fearsome hooks in the centre of every sucker, thought to be the cause of the circular scars seen on the bodies of sperm whales *Physeter macrocephalus*. Little is known about the life of either of these monsters, but sperm whales and sleeper sharks *Somniosus* are known to prey on them.

The ocean's largest ray is the manta ray *Manta biro-stris*, with a 'wingspan' of up to 9.1m (37ft) recorded. Like the whale and basking sharks, it's a filter feeder.

The sharks and rays are cartilaginous fish, but the largest bony fish is thought to be the ocean sunfish *Mola mola*. A sunfish measuring 4.3m (14ft) from fin to fin, 3.1m (10ft) long and weighing about 2,235 kg (4.927lb) collided with a boat off Bird Island on the Queensland coast of Australia. The beluga sturgeon *Huso huso* is a rival for the title. In 1827, a specimen caught in the Volga Estuary was 7.3m (24ft) long and weighed 1,474kg (3,250lb).

The longest bony fish is the king-of-herrings or oarfish *Regalecus glesne*. One hit by a steamship in the nineteenth century was 13.7m (45ft) long. It is thought the oarfish is a possible identity for the fabled 'sea serpent'.

The largest sea turtle is the leatherback turtle *Dermochelys coriacea* with the largest recorded specimen being 2.54m (8.3ft) long and weighing 865kg (1,907lb). It was caught alive in Monterey Bay, California. This species migrates huge distances between the tropics where it breeds and temperate seas where it feeds on jellyfish, and it dives deep.

Unlike most other reptiles it is able to regulate its body temperature and conserve heat. It is thought leatherback turtles could well be responsible for the sightings of 'sea serpents' off the west coast of Britain.

The ocean's largest jellyfish is the lion's mane jellyfish *Cyanea capillata*. A monster measured in Massachusetts Bay in 1865 had a bell diameter of 2.29m (7.5ft) and its tentacles trailed for 36.6m (120ft), making it the 'longest' known animal on Earth. In 2009, a Japanese fishing boat capsized when trying to pull in nets filled with dozens of Nomura's jellyfish *Nemopilema nomurai*, another monster that grows to 2m (6.6ft) across.

The largest known sea urchin is *Sperosoma giganteum*, which is about 30cm (12in.) across, the size of a football. It is found in deep water off Japan and collapses when brought to the surface.

The biggest sponge is a barrel sponge *Xestospongia muta* from the Caribbean. Some specimens are more than 2m (6.6ft) high. Living barrel sponges can be over 2,000 years old, earning them the moniker 'redwoods of the reef'.

RIVER MONSTERS

The arapaima *Arapaima gigas* from the Amazon is often described as the world's largest freshwater fish, with claims of fish up to 4.5m (15ft) long and weighing 200kg (440lb) – but the world's giant catfish can be bigger. The Mekong giant catfish *Pangasianodon gigas* has been reliably weighed at 350kg (772lb) and measured up to 3m (10ft) long, and a specimen of the Chao Phraya giant catfish *Pangasius sanitwongsei*, also from Indochina and caught at Loei, has been credited with a weight of about 300kg (661lb). The European wels *Silurus glanis*, another giant catfish species, is also in contention. Anglers have brought in wels up to 3m (10ft) long, but there are claims of monsters up to 4.3m (14ft). In 1856, a report from the River Dienpr in the Ukraine described a wels 5m (16.4ft) long and weighing 306kg (675lb). The European species also tends to be bulkier than its Asian relatives, so it might turn out to be a record holder.

However, there is one more freshwater fish to consider: a cartilaginous fish, the giant freshwater stingray *Himantura chaophraya*, which lives in the larger rivers of Southern Asia, such as the Mekong. Specimens have been landed that weigh 500–600kg

(1,102–1,323lb) and are up to 4.6m (15ft) long. This has led some authorities to suggest this giant is the world's largest freshwater fish. Unfortunately, all these Asian species are critically endangered due to the degradation of their natural environment.

WORLD'S MOST VENOMOUS ANIMALS

The box jellyfish *Chrionex flackeri* may not look much – in fact, you would be hard-pressed to see it at all. Its box-like body is transparent, almost invisible in the sea, but trailing below are the world's deadliest tentacles, each one armed with up to 50 million stinging cells or nematocysts that work like tiny harpoons on coiled springs. When touched, the spring uncoils and the stinging cell delivers the most powerful venom known to man. It attacks the nervous system, stops the heart, damages skin cells and bursts red blood cells. Victims describe it as unbelievably painful and many do not survive an attack; there have been over 5,500 deaths since the 1950s. The box jelly lives in the waters of the Indo-Pacific region, where local folk have discovered a novel way to escape being stung: they wear tights in the water! Apparently it prevents the discharged sting cells from reaching the skin. Scientists have also discovered that as long as they keep a patient on a ventilator, the venom eventually wears off. It means that in the past people may have died unnecessarily. It's also led to a revolutionary technique in heart surgery. Instead of stopping the heart with the dangerous drugs used currently, it might be possible to do this with box jellyfish venom, therefore incurring no damage to the heart.

Another Indo-Pacific hazard is the blue-ringed octopus *Hapalochlaena*. There are three living species and all are small, no bigger than a chicken's egg, but all are deadly. Each has a bite that delivers a powerful neurotoxin that causes respiratory failure and very quickly death. There's no antidote. Like the box jelly, the blue-ringed octopus is almost invisible. Normally it's so well camouflaged it blends in with its background, but when provoked it turns pale yellow so the bright blue rings on its body stand out. It's a warning: the little octopus will attack. Its venom is not all its own work. Symbiotic bacteria living within the octopus's body, especially in the tentacles, manufacture the neurotoxins.

The marbled cone shell *Conus marmoreus* is a pretty marbled-coloured sea snail, but beware, this little beauty packs an extraordinary punch. One drop of its venom is enough to kill twenty people. Symptoms include intense pain, numbness and a tingling sensation in the skin, but they can worsen to muscle paralysis, vision disturbances and respiratory failure. Only thirty deaths have been recorded, but if you should pick one up and venom is injected, there's no known antidote.

The stonefish *Synanceia* is another master of disguise. Its camouflaged body blends in almost imperceptibly with corals, rocks and seaweeds and the danger is accidentally standing on one. Its dorsal fin spines deliver venom that causes such intense discomfort it has been described as the worst pain in the world. Other symptoms include shock, paralysis and tissue damage, and, if a victim fails to receive medical attention within a couple of hours, the outcome could be death. It is found in the Indo-Pacific region from the Red Sea to Queensland, Australia, where it's considered the most deadly fish in the ocean. It also makes very expensive sashimi called *ozoke*.

The world's most venomous snake is the inland taipan or fierce snake *Oxyuranus microlepidotus*. It is found in the outback of central Australia where, despite its formidable reputation, it hasn't been responsible for a single human death, as all known victims have been treated successfully with an effective anti-venom. Nevertheless, this is one dangerous snake. The amount of venom in a single bite is said to be enough to kill a hundred people, making its venom at least fifty times more potent than that of a king cobra *Ophiophagus hannah* and a hundred times more than an eastern diamondback rattlesnake *Crotalus adamanteus*. Neurotoxins disrupt communication between nerve cells, leading to paralysis and death within forty-five minutes of being bitten. Two close relatives – the coastal taipan *Oxyuranus scutellatus* of northern Australian coasts, and a newly discovered Central Ranges taipan *Oxyuranus temporalis*, are almost as deadly.

The king cobra of southern Asia is the world's longest venomous snake. It grows up to 5.6m (18.5ft) long and its venom is generally used to subdue its main prey – other snakes. When disturbed it will strike out at anything it perceives as a threat, including us. The venom is not especially potent but this snake pumps five times more into its victim than, say, a black mamba. A single bite can kill a human.

Most scorpions have painful stings which are not serious but the death stalker scorpion *Leiurus quinquestriatus* is one of the exceptions. Its venom has a cocktail of neurotoxins that cause intense pain, but it is unlikely to kill a healthy adult – mainly old people, children and the infirm are at risk.

The Brazilian wandering or banana spider *Phoneutria* is considered the most venomous spider on Earth and is responsible for more human deaths than any other species. Its venom contains potent neurotoxins and high levels of serotonin which are responsible for indescribable pain. It also causes priapism – uncomfortable, rock-hard erections that last for several hours and can lead to impotency. As its name suggests, this spider is on the move rather than remaining in a web, although it hides in houses, shoes and cars by day, emerging at night. Fortunately, about one-third of cases show bites without envenomation. However, this species is unusually fierce and will press home an attack rather than scuttle away like other spiders. There is an antidote, but it must be given soon after being bitten.

Funnel-web spiders *Atrax* and *Hadronyche* are found in gardens and forests around Australia. Males are more venomous and tend to attack more often, and because they roam around at mating time they're more likely to be encountered. Symptoms from a bite include salivating copiously, muscle twitch spasms, a speeding heart and a drop in blood pressure, but anti-venoms are widely available. Curiously, funnel spider venom is more toxic to primates than other animals, even though the only primates in Australia are people and they colonised the island continent about 50,000 years ago, insufficient time for there to be an evolutionary link.

BAD TO EAT

At about 7 o'clock on the evening of the 26 March 2009, seven men entered a restaurant in the Yamagata Prefecture in Japan and sat down to a meal of puffer fish sashimi and lightly grilled soft roe. The restaurant owner was inexperienced in preparing puffer fish and at about 8 o'clock the consequences of his inexperience were beginning to be felt. The men first complained of a pins-and-needles sensation, and were rushed to hospital. By the time they got there, two were in a serious condition: one was unconscious and the other had dilated pupils and was in a dazed state. The other five men had milder symptoms. The men were the victims of tetrodotoxin poisoning from eating badly prepared *fugu*, and they were lucky to be alive. Tetrodotoxin is a neurotoxin found in the liver and skin of puffer fish or blowfish (Family: Tetraodontidae). It attacks the nervous system and can end with the death of the victim. As a consequence, puffer fish are considered the second most poisonous vertebrates in the world.

The flesh of some tropical and sub-tropical species of triggerfish, such as the titan triggerfish *Balistoides viridescens*, together with large species of barracuda *Sphyraena*, moray eels (Family: Muraenidae), snapper (Family: Lutjanidae), parrotfish (Sub-family: Scarinae), groupers (Sub-family: Epinephelinae) and amberjacks *Seriola*, can sometimes be poisonous. They carry toxins acquired from dinoflagellates, such as *Gambierdiscus toxicus*. The dinoflagellates are eaten by herbivorous fish, which, in turn, are consumed by fish-eating fish. The poisons build at each stage in the food chain, so predators high in the chain have large amounts in their tissues. The toxins cause the food-borne illness ciguatera and are heat-tolerant, so can't be destroyed during cooking. They cause vomiting, diarrhoea, hallucinations, numbness and can be transferred during sexual intercourse. The symptoms can last for several weeks or maybe even years.

The flesh of the Greenland sleeper shark *Somniosus microcephalus* is poisonous due to the toxin trimethylamine oxide. It produces symptoms similar to extreme drunkenness. The flesh of this shark is considered a delicacy in Iceland and Greenland, but it has to be first boiled with several changes of water or buried in the ground, fermented for five months and dried to produce Kæstur Hákari.

Brightly coloured poison dart frogs (Family: Dendrobatidae) announce that they're unpalatable to predators with vivid skin colours. They eat insects, including beetles (Family: Melyridae) containing lethal alkaloids that act as nerve poisons. They then sequester and concentrate these poisons, which are stored in and secreted through glands in the skin. If smeared on fingers and taken accidentally into the mouth they can be fatal and are some of the most deadly substances known to man. In fact, the golden poison frog *Phyllobates terribilis* is deemed the most poisonous vertebrate on Earth. At any one time, it might only secrete about one milligram (0.000035oz) of poison, but this is enough to kill up to twenty people.

The variable pitohui *Pitohui kirhocephalus* and hooded pitohui *P. dichrous* are birds from New Guinea which have a similar poison in their skin and feathers as poison dart frogs have in their skin. Like the frogs, they sequester the toxins from beetles in their diet, probably from the genus *Choresine*. They are thought to be a chemical defence against ectoparasites, as well as predators. The birds are brightly coloured, which might serve as a warning to any predators that use eyesight to detect their prey, such as tree snakes and raptors. Local people call them 'rubbish birds' because they are no good to eat. And the pitohuis are not alone in having toxins. Two other New Guinea birds – the blue-capped ifrita *Ifrita kowaldi* and the little shrikethrush *Colluricincla megarhyncha* acquire poisons, probably from the same beetles.

The crested rat *Lophiomys imhausi* lives in wooded valleys in East Africa where it defends itself in a unique way, at least for a mammal. It gnaws the roots and bark of *acokanthera* – known as the 'poison arrow tree' – to extract the poison ouabain. It then mixes the poison with its saliva and works it into a special patch of hollow hairs on its flanks. If attacked, the long fur on its flanks parts to expose a black-and-white pattern around a leaf-like patch of the poison-infused hairs. It is as if the rat is daring the predator to bite it. If it does, it won't live for long: it'll die of heart failure. It's the first known example of a mammal employing a plant toxin to make it poisonous to predators.

Some populations of the spur-winged goose *Plectropterus gambensis*, which is found in wetland areas in sub-Saharan Africa, have poisonous flesh and are dangerous for people to eat. These geese generally feed on plant matter, but a population in The Gambia also swallows blister beetles (Family: Meloidea). These beetles are related to Spanish fly *Lytta vesicatoria*, the beetle that produces the toxin catharidin, which causes a swelling of the genitalia and was once used by people as an aphrodisiac. The toxin finds it way into the bird's flesh, and people eating them have been known to die.

In some regions migrating quail *Coturnix coturnix* are poisonous to eat, something that was noted by the physicians of ancient Greece and Rome. Most are not poisonous, but those migrating on the western flyway are poisonous in northern Algeria and southern France on their northward spring migration, while those on the eastern flyway, in Greece and south-west Russia, are poisonous on their southerly autumn migration. Those on the central flyway, to and from Italy, are not poisonous at any time of the year. The source of the poison is still unknown, although the seeds of the annual hedgenettle or woundwort *Stachys annua*, a member of the mint family, may be responsible.

A meal of 30–90g (1–3oz) of polar bear *Ursus maritimus* liver is enough to kill a person. It contains exceptionally high levels of vitamin A, as do the livers of many animals that live in polar regions. The first record of people becoming ill from eating polar bear liver was in 1596, when an expedition visited Novoya Zembla. The first death from vitamin A poisoning to attract medical attention was that of Swiss scientist Xavier Mertz, who was on an expedition in the Antarctic in 1913. The expedition lost its food supplies, so the team was forced to eat their husky sled dogs, but Mertz ate too many of their livers. The halibut *Hippoglossus*, the world's largest flatfish, and Arctic bearded seals *Erignathus barbatus* also have livers with high levels of vitamin A.

POISONOUS AND VENOMOUS

Some of the animals mentioned are 'poisonous', which is significantly different from 'venomous'. Generally, venomous animals use toxins to capture prey, while poisonous animals use toxins to ensure they are not on the menu. It means you eat poisons, or absorb them through the skin, and are injected with venoms. So, a frog or toad is poisonous, but a scorpion, rattlesnake or wasp is venomous.

Northern Australia's floodplain death adder *Acanthophis praelongus hawkei* ambushes frogs. It injects them with venom, but what it does next depends on the species of the frog and how poisonous it is. The rocket frog *Litoria nasuta*, for example, relies on a prodigious leap to escape snakes and is relatively non-toxic, so if it catches one the snake gobbles it down immediately. The marbled frog *Limnodynastes convexiusculus* secretes a glue-like mucus on its skin when caught, but this dries out after about ten minutes so the snake waits for that length of time before swallowing it. Dahl's aquatic frog *Litoria dahlii* is very toxic to snakes. If swallowed, it can kill a snake within twenty minutes, but again its toxins break down within thirty to forty minutes of the frog's death. The snake bides its time, waiting for about forty minutes before eating it.

The Komodo dragon *Varanus komodoensis* was once widespread across Australasia, feeding on the megafauna of the region, but once that disappeared these giant lizards were gradually isolated on Indonesian islands, where a relict population continues to grow to exceptional sizes because it has no competitors. The dragons once ate large herbivores, such as dwarf elephants, but nowadays they eat whatever they can find on the islands – mostly carrion and free handouts, though they do have a predatory streak. They ambush prey – feral goats and water buffalo – and their bite is more subtle than powerful. Their saliva is spiked with virulent bacteria, which means a bite from a dragon could be fatal due to blood poisoning. All the dragon need do is bite and then wait for the prey to die, but that's not all. Researchers at the University of Melbourne found that dragons have venom glands in the lower jaw. When the dragon grabs, bites and holds on tight, it delivers venom similar to that of the gila monster, a venomous lizard that lives in the deserts of south-west North America. They believe that the venom could well contribute to the prey's demise, due to a widening of blood vessels and a prevention of blood clotting, causing a loss of blood pressure and inducing shock. Coupled with blood loss, the victim dies a slow death, only to be torn asunder and the pieces swallowed whole. Komodo dragons, it seems, have access to poisons and venom.

ALLERGIC TO LORISES

The slow loris *Nycticebus coucang* from Indonesia is neither poisonous nor venomous but it does have something that has a venom-like effect. It produces a secretion from a gland on its arm, which it licks and mixes with saliva to create a noxious substance to groom into its fur. In tests it repelled potential predators, such as clouded leopards *Neofelis nebulosa* and sun bears *Ursus malayanus*. Female lorises also spread the secretion over the fur of their offspring to afford them protection too. If a person should threaten a loris, it will lick the gland before it bites, delivering the secretion into the wound. To maximise the effect it doesn't let go. Analysis of the secretion has revealed it to be similar to the allergen in domestic cat dander. It causes local swelling, most probably an allergic reaction, but the only known human death was due to anaphylactic shock.

NATURAL MEDICINES

Chimpanzees *Pan troglodytes* in East Africa treat themselves with the same medicinal plants as local people, and they have their own natural medicine chest. They carefully select and eat whole the folded leaves of *Aspilia*, a member of the sunflower family, which contain a potent antibiotic, antifungal and worming agent. They collect them around dawn, when the leaves have the maximum quantity of antibiotic, and when they fold them they create small perforations through which the chemical can ooze out as the leaf passes through the gut – a kind of time-release mechanism. Chimpanzees with tummy aches due to internal parasites also eat the leaves of *Lippea*, which contain chemicals which are effective against parasites. They also eat the leaves of *Antiaris toxicaria*, which has anti-tumour properties; *Cordia abyssinica*, anti-malarial and antibacterial; *Ficus capensis*, antibacterial; *F. natalensis*, anti-diarrhoea; *F. urceolaris*, de-worming agent; and over twenty additional medicinal plants.

When rhesus macaques *Macaca mulatta* have an upset tummy, they eat one or two leaves of the grass *Cynodon dactylon*, and then vomit to ease the discomfort.

In Uganda, domestic goats *Capra aegagrus hircus* self-medicate with the leaves of *Albizia anthelmintica*. They contain a chemical that rids the goats of parasitic worms.

Black-handed spider monkeys *Ateles geoffroyi* have a medicated back-scratcher. They rub crushed and chewed leaves containing toxins into their fur and those hard-to-get-at places.

The biggest surprise is the self-medicating insects that live in North America. The woolly bear caterpillars of the tiger moth *Grammia incorrupta* are infested with the larvae of parasitic tachinid flies and switch from their normal food plants to the Arizona popcornflower *Plagiobothrys arizonicus*, whose leaves are loaded with toxic alkaloids, to avoid infestation. Those that eat these leaves have a 20 per cent better chance of survival. Similarly, the caterpillars of Ranchman's tiger moth *Platyprepia virginalis* increase their likelihood of surviving an infestation of parasitic flies by switching from bush lupine to poison hemlock. Curiously, the parasite does well too, so they both survive.

The caterpillars of monarch butterflies *Danaus plexippus* feed on several species of milkweed plants. Some plants contain poisons, such as cardenolides, while others are not so noxious. The butterflies lay their eggs on both. The larvae on poisonous plants sequester the noxious substances to make themselves unpalatable to birds, and this is passed on to the adult butterflies during metamorphosis. The butterflies have brightly coloured wings, primarily in black, orange and white, to warn birds that they are poisonous, and it was always thought that the butterflies deposit their eggs on the most toxic plants to give themselves maximum protection against predators, but there could well be another explanation. The caterpillars are plagued by a gut parasite *Ophyrocystis elektroscirrha*, which persists when they pupate and become adult butterflies, and could lead to death. It also means any surviving female butterfly could pass on the parasite when she lays her eggs. However, an infected female is a little more cunning. She has a backup plan. She lays her eggs on the most toxic milkweeds so, although she has not saved herself, she medicates her offspring.

CHEMICAL WARFARE

Gas warfare is waged by a species of African ant *Crematogaster striatula* in the forests of Cameroon. It produces a venomous vapour, like a poisonous gas cloud, from its stinger, so attacking ants can wait at a safe distance while their victim is first paralysed and then dies. It is then hauled back to the nest.

The bombardier beetle *Brachinus* fires a rapidly pulsed stream of boiling hot and noxious chemicals from the tip of its abdomen, and can swivel its rear end to hit attackers coming from any direction.

The short-horned lizards *Phrynosoma* of North America squirt blood from their eyes to deter predators, such as coyotes and foxes.

The stingless winter ant *Prenolepis imparis* of northern California is a survivor. It functions in cold weather, when all other ant species batten down for the winter, and can even deal with invading Argentine ants *Linepithema humile*, which seem set to take over the rest of the Mediterranean world. The winter ants manufacture a poison which is dispensed when the ant is under extreme duress. One drop of the whitish fluid is enough to dispatch an Argentine ant. Not only that, but the winter ants are competing favourably with the Argentine invaders for access to aphids, starving out the aliens.

The golden orb web spider *Nephila antipodiana*, a common species in tropical Asia, uses a chemical weapon to deter ants from invading its web and threatening its life. It laces the strands of the web, especially any anchor lines, with 2-pyrrolidinone, the same toxic substance made by gypsy moth caterpillars *Lymantria dispar* to prevent ants from attacking.

The hagfish (Family: Myxinidae) ranks as one of the most disgusting animals on Earth. This eel-shaped creature, which has a cranium but no backbone and no jaws, produces copious amounts of slime. If placed in a 20-litre (5-gallon) bucket of water, it will turn the water into a sticky slime in a few minutes. It uses this slime, which is more than just a gel, in a variety of ways. It can clog the gills of any fish predator, and if it is grabbed by anything else – a bird or a marine mammal – the hagfish can tie itself into an overhand knot that is worked from the head to the tail, scraping off slime as it goes and freeing the hagfish from its captor. It acquires its own food either by eating marine worms or by scavenging on dead animals, sometimes much bigger than itself. It will coat the carcass with slime to exclude any competitors and use the overhand knot in reverse, from the tail to the head, to gain extra purchase when ripping off pieces of flesh. It often burrows into a large carcass, eating it from the inside out, and if can't stuff enough food into its mouth it can absorb nutrients directly through its skin and gills.

CHEMICALLY CONTROLLED ANTS

Queen black garden ants *Lasius niger,* and probably the sovereigns of many other social insects whose queen is the main egg-layer, produce a pheromone (a chemical messenger) that suppresses workers from producing eggs. Are they being brainwashed or is there some other signal, wondered researchers at the University of Copenhagen. They found that the queen's eggs were coated with the pheromone suggesting a message was carried that 'the queen is in good health and laying many eggs'. If she dies, or is ill and produces less pheromone, workers begin to develop ovaries and the ability to produce eggs.

Like some medieval power-struggle, ant queens are prepared to compromise their entire realm to retain the throne, according to the Copenhagen ant-watchers. New colonies sometimes have multiple queens in their first year so that numbers of workers build up and the colony is prepared for its first winter. Thereafter, things are not so rosy: the newly hatched workers begin to slaughter the weaker queens on the basis of the quality of the queen pheromone they produce, until only one strong queen remains. The other queens don't take this lying down: they cleverly adjust the number of offspring they produce so queens sharing the crown produce fewer workers, thus conserving energy and postponing the inevitable showdown for the throne.

Argentine ants *Linepithema humile* are notoriously tidy, so much so that they clear away a corpse to the graveyard within forty minutes of the insect dying. A non-moving but very alive ant secretes two key chemicals – dolichodial and iridomyrmecin – on its cuticle to avoid being carted off to the mortuary. These suppress another chemical that is always present in the ant's body, which serves to summon the undertakers. When the animal dies, the first two chemicals evaporate and are not replaced, so the undertaker workers detect the third chemical and the ant becomes an official corpse.

REAL ZOMBIES

The fungus *Ophiocordyceps unilateralis* infests the tropical ant *Camponotus leonardi*, turning it into a zombie. They both live in Thailand's rainforests, where the fungus causes the zombie ant to climb down from its normal habitat of a high tree to bite onto a leaf at a lower elevation with what has been described as a 'death grip'. The remarkable thing is that the death grip occurs at a very precise location. The ant bites on a vein on the underside of the leaf of a sapling. The leaf is on the north side of the plant about 25cm (10in.) from the ground, where there is 94–95 per cent humidity and an air temperature of 20–30°C (68–86°F). This, it turns out, is the prime location for the fungus. When the ant dies, the fungus grows inside and eventually produces a fruiting body that always emerges from the same point behind the head. Spores drop to the ground, creating a 'killing zone' of about one square metre below the dead ant, where other ants are likely to pick up the spores and the cycle continues all over again.

In South and Central America, giant gliding ants *Cephalotes atratus* (named for their ability to glide if they fall) eat bird droppings which contain the seeds that they feed to their larvae – but the droppings are sometimes infested with a nematode parasite *Myrmeconema neotropicum*. The parasite's eggs are taken back to the ants' nest and consumed by the ant larvae. As the larvae grow so do the nematodes and their eggs fill the ants' abdomen, which turns bright red and fattens out to resemble the red and juicy berries the birds like to eat. The ants become very sluggish and hold their berry-like abdomens high (normally an alarm posture for these ants). A thinning of the exoskeleton also makes the abdomens easy to break off, so birds, such as bananaquits *Coereba flaveola*, can pluck them and eat them. In this way the parasite is passed on to its next hosts.

Some European and North American snails, e.g. the land snail *Succinea putris*, eat bird droppings and inadvertently take in the eggs of a parasitic flatworm *Leucochloridium paradoxum*. Once inside its host's body, the parasite hatches and heads for the snail's eyes, which are on extendable stalks. The eyes become greatly enlarged and pulsate, while at the same time the parasite causes the now-zombie snail to head for the highest and most conspicuous place on a tree. The pulsating attracts birds that eat the snail's bulging eyes, and the cycle continues.

The emerald cockroach wasp *Ampulex compressa* of French Polynesia attacks and takes over cockroaches *Periplaneta*. It injects venom that first paralyses the roach's front legs temporarily, so it can't get away or struggle, and then injects more venom into the ganglion in the head (brain) where it blocks the neurotransmitter responsible for the roach's escape reaction. The wasp is then, in effect, in total control of the roach. The wasp then leads the zombie cockroach by pulling on its antennae like a dog's lead to its own nest, where the wasp lays a single egg on the cockroach's body. When the egg hatches, the cockroach becomes fresh meat for the wasp's larva and it eats all the internal organs in an order that keeps the roach alive for the longest possible time, or at least as long as it takes for the wasp lava to pupate. Finally, the adult wasp emerges from the cockroach's body and flies off to find another victim.

CATNAPS

Northern elephant seals *Mirounga angustirostris* sleep as they sink. They spend as little time as they can at the surface, just enough to take a few breaths before diving back down. At first they dive fast and steep to about 150m (500ft) to avoid killer whales *Orcinus orca* and great white sharks *Carcharodon carcharias*, but then drift down in a shallow descent. They roll over on their backs, stop actively swimming and spiral down – what has been called the 'falling leaf phase'. Any seal in shallower water might gently hit the bottom and not notice – it's fast asleep.

Dolphins (Family: Delphinidae) sleep with one half of their brain and one eye closed at a time. It means the other half is alert to dangers and it'll know when to take its next breath. In captivity, dolphins enter a fully asleep state with both eyes closed and their blowhole above the surface. An automatic tail kick ensures they are pushed up to the surface should the blowhole dip below the water. Whether they behave like this in the wild is unknown, although their larger cousin, the sperm whale *Physeter macro-cephalus*, does. It hangs vertically in the water while taking a catnap and may drift down just below the surface – but it'll only sleep for about 7 per cent of its day, usually some time between 6pm and midnight. The Indus river dolphin differs from other species in that, living in fast-flowing water, it needs to be alert and active, so it sleeps in short bursts of between four and sixty seconds.

Humpback whales *Megaptera novaeangliae* sometimes sleep at the surface like gigantic floating logs; this behaviour known appropriately as 'logging'. They often log in groups of three, the whale on the inside sleeping the deepest, the two on the outside more alert and watching for danger. After diving to feed, the whales return to the surface and change places, so one of the others can take its turn to sleep the soundest.

Elephants *Loxodonta* sleep for about four hours a day. Depending on how hassled they feel, half of that is spent sleeping while standing up, while the other half can be while lying on their sides. During this deep sleep they might even snore.

Do insects sleep? Well, maybe. Insects are physiologically different to vertebrate animals like us, so their form of sleep is different. The closest they come to sleep is a state called 'torpor'. If they are active during the day they might be in a state of torpor at night, or vice versa. Generally, the insect is immobile and has a reduced response to any stimuli, but can be aroused rapidly if in danger. There is, however, one type of insect that appears to 'sleep' regularly. Male common blue-banded bees *Amegilla cingulata* in Australia use their jaws to clamp onto a plant leaf or stem at night and let go with their legs, which they fold underneath them. They dangle like this until morning, and on successive nights they'll return to the same spot and repeat the behaviour. Males of some species aggregate at 'sleeping roosts', places where they turn up night after night, and males of many species simply go to sleep in flowers.

THE BIG SLEEP

When most small mammals hibernate, their core body temperature lowers considerably – sometimes down almost to freezing – and their general metabolism slows by 50 per cent for every 10°C (18°F) drop in the ambient temperature. When an American black bear *Ursus americanus* hides away for the winter, its body temperature drops by little more than 6°C (11°F), yet its general metabolism and oxygen consumption drop by 75 per cent. While sleeping through the worst of winter, it takes as few as two breaths per minute, its heart fluttering slightly at each breath to give a heart rate of four beats per minute. It remains in its winter den like this for five to seven months, without feeding, drinking, urinating or defecating, and emerges from hibernation in much the same physiological condition as it went in. In fact, bears lose half as much muscle strength as a person confined to bed rest for the same amount of time, and only 10 per cent of muscle protein despite being technically anorexic for several months. What's more, black bears wander around in the weeks just prior to and immediately after hibernation, feeding normally yet still with a reduced metabolism. These observations mean that the study of the physiological changes during bear hibernation could have implications for long-distance manned space travel, help people with heart defects live a more active life and extend the 'golden hour' after an accident, when treatment is most effective, to a 'golden day' or even a 'golden week'.

Copepods are tiny crustaceans that swim about in the surface waters of the ocean in summer, but in the turbulent Southern Ocean *Calanoides acutus* sits out the winter at depths of 500–3,500m (1,640–11,483ft) in a hibernation-like state called diapause. It doesn't eat or move for six months and its metabolism slows so the crustacean ticks over. The abiding mystery has been how it stays down without constantly swimming and using up precious energy – now scientists believe they've discovered its secret. The copepods graze on diatoms all summer, storing fat for the winter in special oil sacs, and the deeper down they go, the more fat they have, especially polyunsaturated wax esters. The wax esters have the property of turning from a liquid at higher temperatures to a solid at lower temperatures – the key to copepod buoyancy. When the copepods go deeper than 500m (1,640ft) their wax esters solidify, making them more dense and less buoyant. At a particular depth, determined by how much fat they have on board, they become neutrally buoyant, the solid wax acting like the weight belt of a scuba diver. They then remain at this depth throughout the winter. In spring, they actively swim up, and as they hit warmer water the wax melts and becomes less dense, their solid ballast turning into a liquid life jacket.

HOT AND COLD, WET AND DRY

Green tree frogs *Litoria caerulea* in Australia come out at night and sit in temperatures so cold they can hardly move. The reason for this is to get a drink at a time when rainfall drops to zero in parts of northern Australia. The cold frogs hop back into their warm dens in tree hollows and condensation forms on their skin, so they glisten with dew. The water is then absorbed through their skin.

The thorny devil *Moloch horridus* is a lizard that lives in the hot desert interior of Australia, and it has a clever way of collecting water. In between the scales all over its body are tiny channels, no wider than a couple of human hairs. These channel water by capillary action from, say, damp ground under the lizard's belly or dew on its back, to the corner of its mouth. The lizard licks the water away, which causes more to be funnelled towards its mouth. The Texas horned lizard *Phrynosoma cornutum* is thought to harvest water in a similar way.

Tiny narrow-mouthed toads *Microhyla*, which live in Sri Lanka, sit out the driest parts of the year by living in moist elephant dung. Fine-grained cow or buffalo dung won't do; it has to be coarse elephant dung because it has a less homogenous and more complex physical structure. The presence of beetles, termites, ants, spiders, scorpions, centipedes and crickets in the dung indicates that elephant dung is a miniature ecosystem all on its own.

Bats don't like to fly in the rain. They might be airborne during a light drizzle, but they'll avoid being out in a downpour. Raindrops hitting the wings are not important and neither is the additional weight of the waterlogged fur. The reason is that they use twice as much energy as when they're dry. It seems, like most animals, bats get cold in the rain and must work harder to keep warm and therefore to keep flying; a bedraggled bat is likely to be less aerodynamic.

Small birds get very stressed when it rains. The smaller the bird, the more often it must feed, and heavy rain prevents them from foraging so they move to places where there is less rain. Male white-ruffed manakins *Corapipo altera* do this. When long-lasting winter storms move into Costa Rica, they migrate from higher elevations where there's more rain to lower ones where there is less. It was always thought that tropical birds undertook these vertical migrations because of the availability of food, but thanks to research at the University of Western Ontario we now know that part of the reason is rain. Female white-ruffed manakins are bigger and need to eat less often than males so they tend to remain at high elevations all year. Males are smaller and must eat more often, so to relieve their stress they head for drier ground. It's thought that many small animals, such as other small birds and butterflies, might make similar migrations for the same reason.

Rain could be a serious hazard for a small hummingbird, especially when the bird is hovering in front of a flower, but it has a simple but effective way to deal with raindrops: it shakes its head from side to side at extraordinary speed. Using high-speed video cameras, researchers at the University of California at Berkeley found that the local Anna's hummingbird *Calypte anna* turns its head 180° in less than a tenth of second, the acceleration reaching a G-force of 34 (compared to a G-force of 6 for a Formula One racing car); and it's doing this while hovering.

A lone ant flails about in water after heavy rain and eventually drowns, but groups of fire ants *Solenopsis invicta* clump together to form a pancake-shaped raft. One layer of ants is submerged, with trapped air ensuring they don't drown, and another layer clambers on top. They link together by mandibles and claws, like a waterproof fabric. Their grip is extraordinary – the equivalent of a human dangling half a dozen elephants from his wrist. The ant raft drifts about until its passengers find dry land or a tree. In this way the ants survive periodic flooding in their South American rainforest home, or wherever else they happen to be, for fire ants are one of the world's worst invasive alien species.

Toucans are tropical birds with enormous bills, but why should they sport such an extravagant and unwieldy accessory – for courtship perhaps? Well, maybe not. Researchers from Canada's Brock University think they have another answer – to keep the bird cool. Birds do not sweat, much like elephants and rabbits, so to lose heat warm blood is directed to special blood vessels located next to a part of the animal's body which is not insulated, such as ears, legs, or in the toucan's case, its bill, and the heat radiates away. The Brock University team has discovered just how effective the toucan's bill is at cooling the bird's body. They studied the toco toucan *Ramphastos toco* of South America, which has one of the biggest bills relative to its body size: it represents 30 to 50 per cent of the bird's surface area. When the bird is flying, they found that the amount of heat radiated away from its enormous bill is the most ever recorded from any animal. Size for size, four times as much heat is shed from a toucan's bill than from an elephant's ears, for example. The researchers estimate that the toco toucan is capable of ditching 100 per cent of the heat it needs to lose via its bill. In this way, it avoids overheating in the steamy tropical forests in which it lives.

Ochre sea stars *Pisaster ochraceus* are starfish that live on the seashore and are exposed to high temperatures at low tides as the sun heats up the water in their rock pools. They keep cool by taking in cold water at high tides and storing it in fluid-filled cavities in their arms. In this way they can lose up to 4°C (7°F) and prevent their bodies from over-heating. The researchers, from the Bodega Marine Laboratory, who carried out the work, liken it to us drinking 7 litres (2 gallons) of water in the morning to prepare for the high temperatures we might experience at noon.

KEEP OFF MY PATCH!

Caterpillars of the North American arched hooktip moth *Drepana arcuata* defend their territory by dragging their rear end aggressively across a leaf. At the tip of the abdomen is a modified hair, known as an 'anal oar', that scrapes over the leaf surface, and the sound is clearly audible in a quiet environment. They also scrape and drum on the leaf with their mandibles.

All mantis shrimps (Order: Stomatopoda) have an armoured body that not only protects them from predators, but also from other mantis shrimps intent on seizing their burrows and territory. Some species possess a formidable hammer-like claw that has been known to smash glass in an aquarium. If this makes contact with a rival's body armour the result could be devastating, but mantis shrimps survive these battles. How do they do it? It seems their armour absorbs the impact like a punch bag, with up to 70 per cent of the energy lost.

California mantis shrimps *Hemisquilla californiensis* 'rumble' to each other. A group of three males will emit rhythmic rumbles in a synchronised chorus, although each individual has its own 'voice'. Their function is unknown, but at the University of Miami researchers who have been recording their sounds in the wild believe they could be used to attract females or to defend their burrows against intruding males.

Piranhas communicate with sound. Most of the time, they swim around in silence, but should two fish confront one another face to face they give a loud 'bark'. It's one way to avoid a fight. However, if one fish should chase another in a fight over food, it emits a pulsed sound and when it bites its rival it makes a softer croak. The sound is made by vibrating the swim bladder, and the muscles responsible contract an astonishing 150 times a second.

Scientists from London's Natural History Museum discovered a minnow-like fish from Myanmar with fangs made of bone and gave it the scientific name *Danionella dracula* after Bram Stoker's infamous character. The species apparently lost its teeth about 50 million years ago, but now it grows bony protuberances that resemble teeth. The males have large fang-like projections. They spar with each other, their open mouths displaying the fangs, but it's all bluff and they don't draw blood.

Eastern Hermann's tortoises *Eurotestudo boettgeri* with the most black pigment in their carapaces (shells) are more likely to pick a fight with a rival and win. Nobody knows why, but one explanation might be that having more of the black colour means that the tortoise absorbs heat from the sun and has more energy for a fight. They are also bolder when taking a handout from humans.

LOST BABIES

If invading male lions *Panthera leo* oust resident males and take over a pride, they will kill all the offspring sired by the previous lions in order to bring lionesses into heat and make them ready to mate. They'll also chase away any juvenile males. Male lions only look after their own offspring. Male hanuman langurs *Semnopithecus* behave in a similar way.

In a reversal of roles, male wattled jacanas *Jacana jacana* look after the brood and females defend the territory. If a territory-holder is defeated or killed, the incoming female will kill her predecessor's chicks and start a new family with the male.

Female gelada baboons *Theropithecus gelada* in Ethiopia's Simien Mountains terminate their pregnancies if a new male takes over the troop. These monkeys live in groups with several females and offspring lorded over by a single mature male. When a new male ousts the old one, he will kill all the offspring sired by his predecessor. So that a pregnant female does not expend unnecessary energy on a 'doomed' infant, she aborts rather than give birth, and 80 per cent of the pregnant females in the troop will do the same.

REALLY WILD COURTSHIP

About half an hour after sunset, two days before each quarter phase of the Moon, the sea off parts of southern California glows green for as long as forty minutes each night. The organism responsible is the fireworm *Odontosyllis phosphorea*, a marine worm that usually lives on the seabed. At breeding time the worms swim towards the surface and the females produce a green slime that glows in the dark. This attracts male worms and both sexes release their gametes into the luminous green cloud. The bioluminescence might have another function, too. Young worms have been seen to produce green flashes, which are thought to distract predators.

The whine of a mosquito in the bedroom at night is enough to drive anyone crazy, but for other mosquitoes it can be a love song. Male and female *Aedes aegypti* mosquitoes, according to Cornell University research, tune their wing beats to 1,200Hz in a mating duet. The frequency is a harmony of their normal wing beat sound: 400Hz for female and 600Hz for males. If researchers can interfere with these mating duets, they might have another weapon in the armoury against these malaria- and dengue fever-carrying mosquitoes.

Stinkbugs (Family: Pentatomidae) use plant stalks as phone lines to communicate with potential mates or rivals. If they made a noise in the open they'd attract unwelcome guests, such as predators, and if they hid behind vegetation their signal wouldn't go very far, so they've adopted a channel of communication that's special to them. They vibrate their abdomens on the stalk at about 100Hz, each species with a slightly different pattern, and the signal is transmitted for several metres.

The male pond skater or water slider *Gerris gracilicornis* in South Korea creates ripples on the water when courting a female. At first it was thought that this was a pond skater serenade, but the reality is a little more sinister. The female pond skater calls all the shots during mating. Her genitalia are covered by a chastity belt and she's reluctant to open it to all comers. She's very choosy about who will mate with her, but the males have found a way to speed up her decision-making. The ripples are not made to attract the female but to summon predatory fish, and the male will continue to make the ripples until the female is so fearful she gives in. This bullying works best if the female has experience of a predatory attack in the past. The male really plays on her fears to get what he wants.

The male Hawaiian sword-tailed cricket *Laupala cerasina* knows just how to woo a mate. He serenades her, rubs antennae, presents her with a nuptial gift made with his own secretions and then inserts a spermatophore containing his sperm into the female's reproductive tract. It was thought that the gift separated the stingy from the generous, the latter making better fathers, but there's more to it than that. Females who received gifts before mating drained more sperm from the spermatophore than those presented with no gift. It seems the gift primes the female to receive sperm, an unexpected function of these little presents.

The male plant bug *Lygus hesperus* makes his female smell repulsive to other males by lacing the spermatophore that he transfers to her during mating with myristyl acetate, a sexual deterrent or anti-aphrodisiac. This form of passive mate guard ensures that the female remains his, and another male does not usurp him.

The diminutive male golden orb web spider *Nephilengys malabarensis* from Australia plucks his chosen female's web to placate her, for she's a giant in comparison and has a healthy appetite. After insemination, he breaks off the end of the palp that delivers the sperm and leaves it inside the female's genital opening, a kind of chastity belt that excludes the sperm of rival males. The palp also continues to pump in sperm long after its donor has withdrawn. The 'eunuch' then hangs around the female's web to make doubly sure that he's not cuckolded, but more often than not he comes to a sticky end anyway – the female eats him.

The male redback spider *Latrodectus hasseltii*, also from Australia, goes one stage further. First, though, he must placate the female with a courtship ritual that must last for at least a hundred minutes or he risks a premature death. Sometimes he can be usurped by a sneaky male watching from the sidelines, who slips in and mates before any of them know what's happening. If he does get to mate, the male twists his abdomen around and impales it on the female's fangs. With her suitably occupied, he can finish the job, but he pays for it with his life.

Male and female tangle-web spiders *Anelosimus studiosus* engage in a little rumpy-pumpy that includes intense courtship and mock copulation before going for the real thing. Males mature early and hang around the webs of juvenile females not ready to mate, but their prenuptials have some benefits. Playful females are less likely to bite a male's head off when they're eventually ready for sex. However, males who fool around a lot tend to end up exhausted and are less able to fight off the competition; for them, foreplay really doesn't pay off.

Many animals, from insects to birds, can detect ultraviolet A (UVA) light, but now researchers at the National University of Singapore have discovered that the banded phintella jumping spider *Phintella vittata* can detect the more dangerous ultraviolet B (UVB) light, which can cause skin cancer and eye damage in humans. They have found it is an important part of the spider's courtship display, though why it uses UVB light is not clear. One reason could be that the spider is using a communication channel that its predators, such as birds, cannot see. There is an indication, however, that some animals, including at least one species of bird, can detect UVB. The neck feathers of domestic pigeons *Columba livia* reflect UVB light, as well as UVA, so if the spiders are using it to escape this predator they had better be careful! Miniscule insects known as thrips and some species of poison dart frogs may well be able to detect UVB too, as they tend to avoid areas with high levels of the light.

In Central American rainforests, red-eyed tree frogs *Agalychnis callidryas* call to attract females but warn rival males by vibrating the branch they are on. In any wrestling matches that follow, the frog that vibrates most vigorously and for longer tends to win. It is the first tree-living animal known to adopt this method of communication.

It has long been suggested that chameleons are the camouflage kings of the reptile world, but are they? Male chameleons are generally a pale brown or green colour, but with a layer of special skin cells wired directly to the brain they are able to flash vivid green, yellow, pink and even ultraviolet. These dramatic colour changes are known to intimidate rivals and impress females, but they were also thought to be linked to camouflage, to help protect the animal from the prying eyes of bird predators. Working with South African dwarf chameleons *Bradypodion* and using a computer program that replicates the eyes of predators and other chameleons, researchers from Australia and South Africa checked out who could see what. They found that the colours were clearly meant for other chameleons to see, but that birds could see them too, so changing colour is a risky business. They concluded that the chameleon's ability to change colour is mainly for communication, and not related to disguise at all. It's a sexy, but highly dangerous, way to stick out from the crowd.

A female giant panda *Ailuropoda melanoleuca* 'chirps' when she is ready to mate. It's the first time a non-human mammal has been observed to change its tune as a sign it's ready to mate (women's voices are higher-pitched at times of peak fertility). Males find it irresistible, but they too have a special call. They bleat when they go courting, and those that bleat the most frequently tend to win the females. They have higher levels of testosterone and other sex hormones in their blood than those that bleat less rigorously. Female pandas, it seems, are attracted to the more aggressive bleaters and rival males tend to avoid them. Any male suitor that doesn't come up to scratch can receive a barrage of growls, barks and moans from the unimpressed female.

On North America's Pacific coast, the male Anna's hummingbird *Calypte anna* chirps with its tail, and researchers at the University of California at Berkeley have discovered that it makes the sound in an unexpected way. It climbs to over 30m (100ft) and then dives headlong towards the ground at 80km/h (50mph). For most of the way down the tail is folded but at the last moment it opens for just one-twentieth of a second, producing a 'sonic squeak'. The sound's function is to attract females, part of a remarkable display that coordinates sound, colour and movement.

Each summer, crested auklets *Aethia cristatella* gather together in huge breeding colonies on islands off Alaska and Siberia. Ticks and other parasites should plague them, but they have an effective defence. They produce a citrus-like scent from 'wick' feathers, hair-like feathers with hollow cores, located between their shoulder blades. And the scent does more than repel bugs; it seems to be attractive to the opposite sex. During courtship and pair bonding, pairs of auklets rub necks, probably transferring the scent from one bird to the other. It's the first recorded instance of a bird transferring a chemical defence substance to another.

People sometimes say they know their partner so well that they finish their sentences for them, but plain-tailed wrens *Pheugopedius euophrys,* which live on the Antisana volcano in Ecuador, are masters of the skill. The male and female sing a duet during which they alternate syllables so rapidly it sounds as if only one bird is singing. To achieve this, researchers from Ecuadorian and American universities have discovered that each bird learns the entire song, not just its own part, much like some actors do. The female sets the pace and never falters, but the male sometimes makes mistakes. Recordings of brain activity in playback experiments, during which birds listened to songs and duets, showed that duets triggered the greatest activity, an indication that there is probably a brain circuit primed for cooperation. It led the researchers to speculate that this might be present in human brains too.

The male great bowerbird *Chlamydera nuchalis* in northern Australia uses an optical illusion to impress a female. He builds an 'avenue' type of bower, about 1m (about 3ft) long, out of sticks, the sides of which face east and west, and decorates the court-yard between the walls with coloured trinkets called 'gesso' – anything from stones to bones, sticks and shells, but always with a preference for things that are white, grey or green. As part of his courtship routine, the male bird picks up objects from the gesso to show to a potential mate. This is where the illusion is created: large objects are placed at the rear of the gesso and small objects at the front. Large objects appear smaller with distance, so the overall effect is that everything in the gesso is roughly the same size, a phenomenon known to photographers as 'forced perspective'. And research at James Cook University has showed that females are, indeed, impressed with males who produce the best illusions. It's not yet clear why, but it could be that the more uniform displays better hold a female's attention and might well demonstrate qualities in the male that impress the female. It's the first time a non-human animal has been known to alter a visual perspective to be viewed by other individuals; put another way, that's 'art'!

Nerds, don't despair. Clever boys get the girls, at least in bowerbird society. Male satin bowerbirds *Ptilorhynchus violaceus* build avenues of sticks and decorate the ground in between with mainly blue objects, from feathers to flowers and even shotgun cartridges and ballpoint pen tops. Researchers from the University of Maryland tested how clever these males are by introducing red objects into their nests. The birds had to work out how to remove them – remove a transparent cover to get at the red object in order to throw it away or cover up a red object that had been screwed to the floor using leaves. Some birds were able to solve the problems, but others didn't seem to have a clue. It turned out that the smart males attract-ed the most females, the cleverest individuals mating with twice as many females as the slowest problem-solvers. Whether females were selecting males on the basis of their braininess or whether it was some other element of the courtship display, such as a sexy dance, is not clear, but the brainy birds undoubtedly won the most hearts.

Many male animals make themselves bigger and bulkier to intimidate their rivals in order to win the right to mate with females. Ducks, however, just grow bigger penises. Two species have been studied – the lesser scaup *Aythya affinis* and the ruddy duck

Oxyura jamaicensis. During the mating season, the penises of lesser scaup drakes grow about 4cm (1.6in.) longer, and those of ruddy ducks grow 15cm (6in.) longer than normal. It's the first known example in vertebrates of social competition being driven by the size of male genitalia.

The golden-collared manakin *Manacus vitellinus* is a small, mainly yellow, bird that lives in the tropical rainforest of South and Central America. The male performs elaborate courtship dances to impress a potential mate. According to one of the researchers at the University of California at Los Angeles (UCLA), part of his dance is 'like being shot out of a cannon' and he 'sails like an acrobat to land perfectly on his perch'. During his dance, if he moves his feet quicker than any of his rivals he's more likely to attract the attention of the females. The difference between contenders is surprisingly small. Just 30 milliseconds difference will give the faster bird the edge and, if he throws in a few backflips and his heart races from 600 to 1,300 beats per minute, the marriage is in the bag. The high-energy performance, increased heart rate and slick dancing skills are probably seen as good traits in a father-to-be. Inheriting the ability to move quickly would enable the manakin's offspring to escape predators.

Groups of female long-finned squid *Loligo pealeii* arrive in spring and early summer at communal spawning grounds in a variety of locations in the North Atlantic. Each female deposits many egg capsules and mates repeatedly. The males hang about in schools, waiting for their chance to mate, but should the suckers at the tips of their two long tentacles touch an egg case their behaviour changes abruptly. The male turns on his nearest neighbour and attacks him in a highly aggressive fight, and the most aggressive fighters gain the greatest number of copulations with females. The chemical on the egg case, which is a contact pheromone, appears to channel a male's competitive aggression to where it is most likely to result in fertilisation. Females gain by receiving sperm from the most vigorous males.

Female sperm whales *Physeter macrocephalus* rule the roost. The solitary males were once thought to take over a harem of females at breeding time, but now researchers from Dalhousie University have discovered that females appear to 'approve' of some males, while 'rejecting' others. Knowing this explains what happened to sperm whale populations during widespread commercial whaling. The whalers thought that if they left a single male he would mate with the females and produce more whales, so they could slaughter all the other males in the area. However, the pregnancy rates of the females dropped significantly and this continued long after commercial whaling was banned. From this research, it appears that the surviving females were unimpressed with the male they had been left with and failed to breed, so the impact of whaling had implications far beyond the number of whales killed.

In their breeding grounds in the tropics and subtropics, male humpback whales *Megaptera novaeangliae* sing the most incredibly long and complex songs. Like bird song, they consist of repeated patterns, but they last for thirty minutes or more. The function of the songs is still unknown, despite many decades of research, but a singer could be communicating with other males or with females. While the whale remains motionless in the water, singing, sometimes a younger whale will come and listen, like a pupil with his maestro. Males also band together, so the songs might be a rallying call for larger males to gain a posse of young helpers. Parties of males fight hard and long over females, so having a gang backing you up might be intimidating for the opposition; when things do come to blows there's more muscle available. Fights can be bloody, with whales ramming each other, slamming each other with tails and flippers, blowing angry bubbles and attempting to drown the opposition by covering his blowhole. What the younger whales gain, except for experience or the odd chance to mate when nobody's looking, is not clear, but the bigger males are choosy about whom they chase. The bulls go after the larger females: an additional half-metre (1.6ft) in length equates to four more male escorts. The reason is that an extra metre (3.3ft) in a female's length results in an extra one-third of a metre (one foot) in her calf's length; so larger females probably have stronger calves, a good investment opportunity for a male. Females are equally choosy, selecting the winning male amongst the battling escort whales. As for the unlucky males, they find a space and start singing again.

ODD COUPLES

Oral sex is not common in the animal world. We humans practise fellatio, as do our closest relatives the bonobos *Pan paniscus*, but now a bat has joined our exalted ranks. The male short-nosed fruit bat *Cynopterus sphinx* from south-east Asia first attracts a female by making a tent from fan-palm leaves. If he's successful, the pair indulge in a bout of mutual grooming, followed by the male entering the female from behind. Then, the female turns her head and licks the male's penis; the longer she licks, the longer copulation lasts. For each second of licking, copulation is extended by six seconds. Why they do this must be pure speculation, but the Chinese research team who observed this behaviour have suggested it might prolong the male's erection, it may act as a lubricant and might also reduce the chances of contracting a sexually transmitted disease because of the anti-microbial properties of saliva. On the other hand, say the researchers, they might just be sexually playful, like we are.

Two male mute swans *Cygnus olor*, born in 2002 at the Abbotsbury Swannery in southern England, have taken up with each other for several years in succession. In the herd of 1,000 swans they are the only same-sex pair. Each summer, they build a nest and take it in turns to sit on it and defend it from other swans. All they need is some eggs to appear and their lives would be complete.

The deep-sea squid *Octopoteuthis deletron* lives a normally solitary life between 400 and 800m (1,312– 2,625ft) down in the darkness of the Monterey Submarine Canyon off the Californian coast. Finding a mate is not easy down there so a male squid will mate with whatever squid it chances upon – male or female. They don't seem to care. The researchers from the Monterey Bay Aquarium Research Institute, who observe these characters from remote-controlled submersibles, believe it is more cost-effective for a male squid to waste sperm on a same-sex mating than evolve an elaborate courtship display to woo a female rarely encountered in the deep sea.

FIDDLER IN THE MUD

Adult male fiddler crabs *Uca* have one claw considerably bigger than the other and often brightly coloured. It is waved to attract females as much as twenty times from the moment the male spots the female. Other males will wave their claws, even if they can't see the female, by eavesdropping on the claw-waving behaviour of their neighbours. And when several crabs are waving at the same time, they up their rate of waving by as much as 30 per cent to try to stand out from the crowd.

The male fiddler crab can be dishonest. His huge claw is used not only for courtship, but also to resolve territorial disputes. Crabs with the strongest and most impressive claws win the right to occupy a choice patch of mud by yanking the resident from his burrow. Closing force and pulling power are paramount. Occasionally, fiddler crabs lose their large claw and must re-grow it, but the new claw is usually weaker than the original. The male, though, bluffs it. When looking to take over a territory he'll search for a resident male with a smaller claw and wave his new claw menacingly, even though it is lighter and has much less power. The smaller resident usually gives up without a fight, so the bluff has worked. When he is defending his burrow, however, he'll first try to bluff his way out; if his bluff is called, he'll inevitably lose the ensuing fight.

Male fiddler crabs on their exposed mud arenas often suffer heat stress and hunger, what with all their arm-waving, and their enormous claw is actually a hindrance when foraging for food. Could it, wondered scientists from the University of Texas, have another function that might make it even more worthwhile? They found that it has: to keep cool. Crabs with intact claws cool down quicker than those with missing or damaged claws. Heat from the body is transferred to the claw and then lost into the surrounding air by convective heat transfer. It means the males are able to remain on the surface for longer, performing their vigorous waving displays and foraging for food.

Baby fiddler crabs *Uca pugnax* and *U. pugilator* at Tybee Island, Georgia, USA, hide in empty shells of the marsh periwinkle *Littoraria irrorata*, much like hermit crabs, except that they don't carry the shell on their back.

BRINGING UP BABY

The mother seed beetle *Mimosestes amicus* is plagued by parasitic wasps *Uscana semifumipennis*. They drill into her eggs and deposit their own offspring inside, but she has a cunning plan: she hides some of her eggs underneath a living shield. She stacks her eggs so that the more viable ones are underneath and those that are less viable are on top; in fact, the top ones have far fewer nutrients in the yolk than those underneath. So, when the wasp comes along and drills into the uppermost eggs, the wasp grubs actually end up starving, while the diligent beetle mother's eggs are safely developing down below.

A newly discovered Madagascan frog *Blommersia angolafa* is the first amphibian known to lay its eggs and rear its tadpoles in the water that accumulates in dead palm leaves on the forest floor.

The female European cuckoo *Cuculus canorus* gives her offspring a head start by incubating her egg for twenty-four hours inside her own body before laying it in the host bird's nest. This ensures the cuckoo chick hatches before its foster parent's own progeny. The chick then ejects the other eggs from the nest so it is the sole recipient of food brought back by the unwitting foster parents, who may be much smaller than their 'offspring'.

The chicks of songbirds (Suborder: Passeri), much like human babies learning to talk, 'babble' before they sing properly. The part of the brain involved in babbling, however, is very different to that responsible for adult songs and singing. It means the transition from babbling to fully fledged song is not simply a refinement of an existing brain circuit, but a switch from one network to another. Looking at the wider picture, the researchers from the Massachusetts Institute of Technology speculate that parts of the developing vertebrate brain (and that includes human brains) could contain components related specifically to youthful behaviour.

The purple-crowned fairy wren *Malurus coronatus* from tropical Australia is not only a cooperative breeder but is also the accountant of the bird world. Cooperative breeding, during which young birds help older birds to rear chicks, was always thought to be a partly selfless act in which their only gain is to ensure at least some of their genes survived, but research at Monash University has revealed that in the case of fairy wrens the behaviour is far from altruistic. Helpers weigh up carefully any advantages they might gain, especially whether their chances of inheriting the breeding territory are good, as well as assessing how many helpers they might inherit from the brood they help to bring up. In effect, they are helping to feed and nurture their own future assistants.

Pairs of black kites *Milvus migrans* in south-west Spain decorate their nests with rubbish, but only if it is white. They ignore litter of other colours, prefer-ring white materials that can be seen from some distance away. The litter says to any bird intent on stealing from the nest or attempting to take over the nest site, 'Don't mess with us!' It is a sign of fitness. Ecologists at the Doñana Biological Station monitored the birds and found that those with the whitest litter had their nest sites closer to marshland and the best food supplies, and were the most successful breeders. Birds with poor territories, as well as old and young birds, had plain nests with no litter, and the other kites bothered them continually with up to six raids in an hour.

The penguin that breeds the furthest south is the emperor penguin *Aptenodytes forsteri*. Its colonies are on the sea ice that surrounds the Antarctic continent, and in order for chicks to fledge in the brief southern summer, breeding occurs during the cold, dark winter, when a huddle of 5,000 birds endures temperatures as low as −50°C (−58°F) and winds blowing at 200km/h (125mph). For the first nine weeks, the eggs rest on the male bird's feet, enveloped in a roll of skin and feathers 70°C (126°F) warmer than the air outside. The male doesn't eat and loses nearly half his body weight before the female returns to relieve him on brooding duty, at just about the same time as the chick starts to hatch.

Great white pelicans *Pelecanus onocrotalus* normally hunt cooperatively for fish, but in areas where stocks are low, such as Dassen Island off the coast of South

Africa, they've taken to eating other birds. Their unfortunate neighbours on nearby Malgas Island are cape gannets *Morus capensis*. On this island, the fish shortage is forcing both nesting parents to go to sea to find food at the same time, so many gannet chicks are unguarded. It's an open invitation for pelicans. Every day they fly in and wander amongst the gannet nests, swallowing cape gannet chicks live and whole. Any bird less than 2kg (4.4lb) is fair game. And, having acquired a taste for bird flesh, the pelicans have taken to raiding nests on their own island, with the chicks of cape cormorants *Phalacrocorax capensis*, kelp gulls *Larus dominicanus*, swift terns *Thalasseus bergii* and African penguins *Spheniscus demersus* bearing the brunt of the pillaging.

Female harp seals *Pagophilus groenlandicus* do not give birth to their pups on any old pack ice; they're quite choosy. They select grey-white ice, which is 15–30cm (6–12in.) thick, or first-year ice, which is 30–120cm (12–50in.) thick. The choice of ice platform is critical, for the pup is weaned and on its own twelve days after its birth. Thereafter, it must remain adrift for another month, when it practises swimming and hunting. It leaves its ice raft at about the same time most of the ice breaks up and melts in spring, so timing is important. If the ice platform is too thin the pup would be pitched into the water too early and probably drown.

Babysitters look after young sperm whales *Physeter macrocephalus* while their mothers dive for food in the Caribbean and Sargasso seas. The Sargasso mothers form a babysitting circle, each taking it in turns to looks after the young, while the young of Caribbean pods, which have fewer mothers, are looked after by a female relative.

In December 2007, field biologists from the University of Pretoria came across an adult king penguin *Aptenodytes patagonicus* defending a skua chick, the penguin's arch enemy. They were on sub-Antarctic Marion Island in the Southern Indian Ocean, where the penguin had probably mistaken a fluffy brown skua chick for a similarly coloured king penguin chick, and adopted it. The chick's parents tried time and again to retrieve their offspring, but the penguin would have none of it. The behaviour is all the more surprising given that adult sub-Antarctic skuas *Catharacta antarctica* are predators that seek out and regularly eat penguin chicks.

On an island in the Galapagos Archipelago, Nazca boobies *Sula granti* (a species of gannet) echo human behaviour: birds abused as chicks turn out to be the most likely birds to become abusers.

Green sea turtle hatchlings *Chelonia mydas* must run the gauntlet of predators across the beach before they reach the sea, but there's still a whole gamut of sharks and other fish waiting for them in the shallows. They must swim as fast and as far as their little flippers will carry them. Initially the hatchlings swim hard using their front flippers, doggy-paddling as they take a breath at the surface. After the first half hour the thrust drops rapidly and then declines more slowly over the next ten hours, levelling off after twelve hours. Looking at oxygen consumption during this dash out to sea, researchers at the University of Queensland discovered that these little hatchlings carry about ten times as much energy in the remnants of their yolk sacs than is needed to reach the relative safety of deep water. It means they could probably survive for up to fourteen days in the open sea without having to feed.

Biologists from Galicia's Marine Research Institute were observing common cuttlefish *Sepia officinalis* mating and spawning in the sea off north-west Spain when they saw something very odd. The female cuttlefish were attaching their eggs to sea grass – but one individual had attached her eggs to a passing seahorse!

ALARM

The crested pigeon *Ocyphaps lophotes* from Australia produces a fluttering whistle when it takes off normally, but when disturbed by a predator the take-off sound is faster, louder and more urgent. Researchers at the Australian National University wondered whether this might act like an alarm call, and carried out some playback experiments. They played recordings of ordinary take-offs and other birds ignored them, but when they played the faster sounds, all flocks took to the air immediately. It is the first non-vocal alarm call to be found in birds.

Blue monkeys *Cercopithecus mitus stuhlmanni* appear to warn others in their troop of the proximity of danger. They have two calls – one for aerial preda-tors, such as eagles, and another for those on the ground, such as leopards – so that other members in the troop know where to look for the threat. In playback experiments by researchers from the University of St Andrews, alarm calls were played to a troop in Uganda. The lead male responded by giving his alarm call about twenty-three times. However, if a young monkey was close to the playback loudspeakers and therefore closer to the perceived 'threat', the male gave his call forty-two times. It was as if he was saying to the youngster, 'Watch out – get away from there!'

Marine iguanas *Amblyrhynchus cristatus* live on the Galapagos Islands, where they feed on green seaweed growing on submerged rocks. They alternate dives of about thirty minutes with basking in the sun to warm up again, but while they're out of the water the iguanas, especially younger animals, are vulnerable to predation by Galapagos hawks *Buteo galapagoensis*. As soon as a hawk appears, the iguanas race for cover, but they also have an early-warning system: they listen for the alarm calls of mockingbirds. The birds spot the hawk long before the iguanas can see it, so as soon as the birds call, the iguanas look up. The closer the lizards are to the hawks' nest sites, the more alert they are. For the ecologists from Princeton University, it came as a surprise that a non-vocal animal like a marine iguana uses an acoustic cue.

African savannah elephants *Loxodonta africana* are afraid of bees. The native bees of southern Africa *Apis mellifera scutellata* are noticeably more aggressive than their European or North American relatives, and even elephants have vulnerable soft parts, such as the belly, behind the ears, around the eyes and inside the trunk. When elephants hear them, they shake their heads and give a 'bee rumble' – a very low-frequency alarm call, the first elephant alarm call to be associated with a particular threat. In a related study, the researchers from Oxford University played the sounds of angry bees to herds of wild elephants and, without exception, herds left the area within ten seconds of hearing the bees. The research is aimed at finding a natural way to deter elephants from raiding crops. So far, planting chillies is the only method that works, but combining this with special fencing that incorporates beehives might be even more effective.

When meerkats *Suricata suricatta* mob a dangerous snake, it could be a practical class on predator recognition for youngsters. Meerkat adults aged about one to two years old tend to mob long and hard, while younger meerkats are less intense. The older animals are thought to be teaching the younger ones by example. It occurs in other aspects of meerkat life.

Young meerkats mimic adults in catching scorpions, babysitting and colony guard duties. It's thought mobbing could be another aspect of social learning at the meerkat school.

THE GREAT ESCAPE

California ground squirrels *Otospermophilus beecheyi* protect themselves and their offspring from snakes, especially rattlesnakes *Crotalus*, by waving their tails and throwing dirt. It's a form of intimidation: tail-waving makes them look bigger and signals aggression, so the snake might have second thoughts on whether it should attack. The curious thing, however, is that squirrels wave their tails even more rigorously in the dark. The reason is that rattlesnakes have sensors on their face which detect infrared radiation (heat). To figure large on the rattlesnake's radar, the squirrel pumps warm blood into its waving tail. Faced with a gopher snake, which has no heat sensors, the squirrel waves a cool tail. The heated tail is the squirrel's way to communicate with its number one enemy, the rattlesnake.

Horned frog *Ceratophrys ornata* tadpoles in Argentina scream underwater. If attacked they emit a loud metallic sound. These tadpoles are aggressively carnivorous and will eat the tadpoles of other species. To prevent cannibalism, they scream if attacked by their own species.

Screeching frogs (Family: Arthroleptidae) in Cameroon have hands like the comic-book character Wolverine. Sharp, claw-shaped bones burst through the skin of their fingertips when threatend. They might also use the system for a better grip when clambering over slippery surfaces.

When a bat pursues the tiger moth *Bertholdia trigona* it's in for a surprise. As it approaches for the kill, the moth suddenly emits a burst of noise that doesn't simply startle the bat, it actually jams its echolocation system, so the moth can fly away undetected.

Fruit flies *Drosophila melanogaster*, and probably most other species of flies, carry out a key feet-shuffle just before they escape from danger. When a predator attacks, the fly detects the movement and 100 milliseconds before it beats its wings it moves its feet so that its body mass is centred over its two middle legs, then it jumps in the opposite direction of the approaching danger. This is an extraordinary bit of anticipation and manoeuvring for a creature with no more than 100,000 neurons in its brain, suggests researchers at San Diego's Neurosciences Institute. It means when swatting a housefly you need to over-shoot to make contact.

Most hoverflies (Family: Syrphidae) mimic the black-and-yellow stripes of wasps in order to dupe predators, but some flies have more vivid wasp-like patterns than others. The reason appears to be in their size. Big flies are the best mimics because birds prefer big, juicy flies. The smaller species are the worst mimics because they are under less pressure to evolve elaborate disguises than the bigger flies.

Moth and butterfly caterpillars have all sorts of ways to avoid being eaten by predators – poison in their body, irritating hairs, camouflage, hiding inside rolled up leaves or producing noxious faeces – but North America's walnut sphinx moth caterpillar *Amorpha juglandis* has the most novel escape plan: it 'whistles'. When a bird pecks at it, the caterpillar forces air through large spiracles on either side of its eighth abdominal segment, producing a high-pitched whistle. Caterpillar-eating birds, such as yellow warblers *Dendroica petechia*, are startled by the sound and jump back or fly away. The sound is the acoustic equivalent of startling eyespots on moth and butterfly wings.

If free-swimming larvae of the sand dollar *Dentraster excentricus* detect mucus from a predatory fish, they split into two and bud smaller clones. The cloned individuals are much smaller than the original larva, closer in size to sand dollar eggs, and are therefore less easy for fish to spot. The process is slow, taking twenty-four hours for a bud to form, and the clones could easily be gobbled up. This is no short-term fix but a long-term strategy to have a larger number of smaller versions of oneself in the water with a better chance of some clones surviving.

The brightly coloured copepods *Anomalocera ornate* and *Labidocera aestiva* are unusually large and, unlike most other copepods that migrate deep down in the ocean during the day, these characters live day and night at the surface, where their bright blue or green colour protects them from harmful UV rays. Being so conspicuous, especially to fish predators, it was unclear how they survived; that is, until a scientist at the University of Texas noticed a rain-like pattern on the sea's surface. He scooped up some of the water and put it in an aquarium. It was packed with copepods. He introduced some plankton-eating fish and watched. To his surprise the copepods escaped the fish's jaws by leaping out of the water, travelling through the air ten to twenty (and sometimes forty) times their own length, so the 3mm (0.1in.) long crustacean might land up to 12cm (5in.) away. The leap occurs when their five pairs of swimming legs beat in rapid succession, pushing the copepod through the water surface and propelling it at speeds of 0.66m/sec. (2.2ft/sec.) in midair, where they somersault at up to 125 revolutions per second, and out of line of sight of any pursuer. And, it works: of eighty-nine leaping individuals in the test tank, only one was caught during the time the high-speed video camera was running. How they achieve these acrobatic feats in such a dense medium as water is unknown.

In deep waters off the coast of the Philippines and along North America's Pacific coast, Scripps Institution of Oceanography scientists have discovered new species of deep-sea marine annelid worms *Swima* that unleash tiny balloon-like 'bombs' that suddenly burst into light with an eerie green glow the moment they separate from the worm's body. Like the ink cloud from a squid or cuttlefish, the green blobs, which are made from modified gill parts, are thought to distract predators so the worm can make good its escape. They're good swimmers, propelled along by long, paddle-like bristles. Some species, e.g. *S. bombiviridis* in Monterey Bay, live near the sea floor 3,793m (12,444ft) deep, while others are closer to the surface, about 400m (1,312ft) above the seabed.

Clusterwink snails are small marine snails that live in clusters on the rocky seashores in Australia. One species *Hinea brasiliana* produces a dazzling flash of bioluminescent green light and it displays it in a novel way. Its pale yellow shell is opaque and at first sight would seem a barrier to light transmission, but it isn't. When a crab or other predator threatens, the sea snail goes off like a burglar alarm. It flashes green, the only colour that's scattered by its shell, spreading light in all directions. In this way the snail appears to look much bigger than it really is, a bio-optical illusion, and it draws attention to itself and, more importantly, to other predators. The snail has put the spotlight on its aggressor, with the hope of drawing in even bigger predators – a second line of defence.

The splendid lantern shark *Etmopterus splendidus* can virtually disappear. It has bioluminescent organs called photophores that glow on the underside of its body. From the perspective of a predator approaching from below, the photophores replace the natural light coming down from the surface, which is absorbed by the shark's body. In effect it has a cloak of invisibility, for it blends in with its background and its silhouette disappears when seen from below. Other deep-sea sharks have similar predator avoidance systems.

Two deep-sea creatures – the octopus *Japetella heathi* and the squid *Onychoteuthis banksii* – are able to change their camouflage at will. They live at a depth of about 600–900m (2,000–3,000ft), where there is barely a glow from the surface. Nevertheless, the two creatures are both transparent. The little light that diffuses from above passes through their bodies, making them invisible to any predators approaching from below. Even their eyes and gut, which cannot be made transparent, are reflective, minimising their silhouette. Many deep-sea predators tend to illuminate their prey with bioluminescence, but the squid and the octopus have an answer to that. If they detect the light from a predator, they rapidly expand their pigment cells and change from the transparent state to an opaque red colour in an instant. Red is invisible in the deep sea.

Discovered in 1998 off the coast of Sulawesi, the mimic octopus *Thaumoctopus mimicus* takes on the characteristics and behaviour of a number of marine creatures, many of which are venomous or dangerous. It impersonates the toxic zebra sole flatfish, venom-spined lionfish, brittle stars, giant crabs, sea anemones, mantis shrimps and sea snakes by configuring its arms into the relevant shapes, copying undulating movements and displaying brash brown-and-white striped patterns. In fact, it mimics the creature that would be the most effective deterrent. If a pair of aggressive and territorial damsel-fish threatens this talented octopus, for example, it mimics the banded sea snake, a predator of damsel-fish. But now a small fish has been seen to mimic the mimic. The black-marble jawfish *Stalix histrio* normally remains close to its burrow in the sand, but a marine biologist from the University of Gottingen filmed one mimicking the colour of the octopus and hiding amongst its arms as it scrambled across the sand. For its part, the octopus ignored its tiny companion. This case of 'opportunistic mimicry' enables the fish to venture far from its burrow in its search for food.

Pods of Blainsville's beaked whales *Mesoplodon densirostris* chatter away with buzzes, clicks and whistles when they dive to 900m (2,950ft) deep, but when they return to the surface they become silent at a depth of about 170m (560ft). It's thought that by going into stealth mode near the surface they avoid drawing attention to themselves, especially when killer whales *Orcinus orca* are about.

Permanent pods of ten or so female sperm whales *Physeter macrocephalus* in the Pacific Ocean some-times join other pods to form much larger clans. In the Atlantic, where the whales are genetically simi-lar to their Pacific cousins, they rarely form larger groups. The reason is thought to be the predatory attention of killer whales. Whale watchers in the Pacific have witnessed at least six attacks on sperm whales by killer whales, but in the Atlantic they've seen none, even though Atlantic sperm whales have been observed more often. The bigger clans in the Pacific are a way for sperm whales to gang up on killer whales and protect themselves and their offspring from the inevitable attacks.

BEE POWER

Honeybees *Apis mellifera* in Japan are vulnerable to attacks by Japanese giant hornets *Vespa mandarinia japonica*. European honeybees, which are kept by Japanese beekeepers because they produce more honey than the local breed, are very susceptible. A single hornet can kill forty bees in a minute, and the ring of pheromones that it daubs around the hive will attract more of its nest mates in an awesome raiding party. A hive of 30,000 bees can be decimated in less than three hours by thirty hornets. Japanese honey-bees, however, unlike their European cousins, fight back. An advance party of 500 will fly out and surround the scout hornet before it can release any phero-mones. They form a tight ball around it and vibrate their wings so that the temperature at the centre of the ball increases to 47°C (117°F), like a convec-tion oven – a behaviour known as 'thermoballing'. The bees can tolerate a top temperature of 48–50°C (118–122°F), but the poor old hornet succumbs at 44–46°C (111–115°F), so the bees win the day.

On the Mediterranean island of Cyprus, however, oriental hornets *Vespa orientalis* tolerate higher temperatures, so the local honeybees cannot perform the same trick; instead, they mob and suffocate their attacker. When a hornet exhales, the plates of its exoskeleton cover its spiracles, and it can only inhale if its abdomen is free to move. The sheer weight of honeybees keeps the plates in place and the spiracles closed, so the hornet cannot breathe. The Cypriot bees also survive to fight another day.

Honeybees guard plants too. Leaf-eating caterpillars have fine hairs at the front end of their bodies that detect air vibrations, such as the wing vibrations of an attacking wasp. The caterpillar stops eating and drops from the plant. But caterpillars are unable to distinguish between marauding wasps and harmless pollinating honeybees, so when a bee comes to drink nectar from a flower the caterpillar drops from the plant. It means the honeybee not only helps to pollinate the plant, but also protects it.

INSECT RECORD-BREAKERS

The world's largest known adult insect is the giant weta *Deinacrida heteracantha*, found only on Little Barrier Island, New Zealand. A specimen was found in 1991 that weighed 71g (2.5oz). However, giant scarab beetles *Goliathus* and *Megasoma* together with the Titan beetle *Titanus giganteus* are likely to knock the weta from top position as more specimens are found. The longhorn beetle *Macrodontia cervicornis* and the Hercules beetle *Dynastes hercules* are contenders for the longest beetle.

The world's longest insect is a stick insect from Borneo. A specimen of *Phobaeticus chani* in London's Natural History Museum has a body 35.7cm (14in.) long, and with its front legs fully extended it is 56.7cm (22in.) long. Other species of the genus *Phobaeticus*, including *P. kibyi*, also from Borneo, which measures up to 54.6cm (21.5in.) long, and *P. serratipes*, from Malaysia, with a length of 55.5cm (21.85in.), could well overtake *P. chani* as more specimens are found.

Queen Alexandria's birdwing *Ornithoptera alexandrae*, a butterfly from Papua New Guinea, and the Atlas moth *Attacus atlas*, both common across the Malay Archipelago, compete for the title of 'world's biggest moth or butterfly'. They both have wingspans of up to 28cm (11in.) and a body length of 8cm (3.2in.). Challengers include the white witch *Thysania agrippina* of Latin America – wingspan 36cm (14in.), and Australia's Hercules moth, with a 35.5cm (13.97in.) wingspan claimed.

The world's strongest insect is Australia's horned dung beetle *Onthophagus taurus*. It can pull 1,141 times its own body weight, the equivalent of a person pulling 80 tonnes or six full double-decker buses.

The world's fastest-running insect is an Australian tiger beetle *Cicindela hudsoni*, which can motor along at 2.5m/sec. or 9.01km/h (5.6mph).

The world's most deadly insects are mosquitoes, especially *Anopheles gambiae*, which transmits the most dangerous malaria parasite *Plasmodium falciparum* amongst humans. The mosquitoes are closely followed by rat fleas *Xenopsylla cheopis*, which carry diseases such as the bubonic plague that can kill within four days; Africa's tsetse fly *Glossina*, which carries sleeping sickness; and South America's kissing bugs *Triatoma infestans* and *Rhodnius prolixus*, which spread Chagas disease.

By its very size, the 4cm (1.6in.) long giant Japanese hornet *Vespa mandarinia japonica* is also considered a deadly insect. Its venom, which attacks the nervous system and damages tissues, is not especially potent but it can deliver large quantities and sting repeatedly. In Japan, forty people die each year due to anaphylactic shock after being stung by giant hornets, making this insect the most dangerous animal in Japan, ahead of bears which kill ten people each year and venomous snakes which kill five.

Another wasp – *Vespa luctuosa* from the Philippines – has the most potent venom of any wasp. Its sting is extremely painful, the venom causing convulsions, a bluing of the skin and red blood cells in the urine. But the insect with the most deadly venom is the harvester ant *Pogonomyrmex maricopa*, a species found in south-western USA. Just twelve stings from this ant can kill a 2kg (4.4lb) rat. In humans, the excruciating pain can last for over four hours, after which it becomes less intense.

The world's most destructive insects must include termites which destroy buildings by eating mainly wood, although as a bank in the northern India town of Arthur discovered, they'll have a go at other assets too. On 19 April 2011, bank officials entered their vaults only to discover that termites had eaten 10 million rupees!

Even more devastating are locusts, especially the desert locust *Schistocerca gregaria*, which consumes vital crops in poor tropical regions. The largest desert locust swarm was estimated to contain 40 billion insects and covered an area of 1,036 sq. km (400 sq. miles). Locust plagues have an impact on the food of one-tenth of the world's human population. They also travel great distances. In 1988, swarms of desert locusts flew in a storm system that took them from West Africa to the Caribbean, a distance of 4,500km (2,796 miles), and many would have flown considerable distances in Africa before their Atlantic crossing. This is the longest known migration of any flying insect.

A tiny trap-jaw ant *Odontomachus bauri*, native to South and Central America, has probably the fastest jaws in the world. It has a spring-loaded catch mechanism that can snap shut at a staggering 230km/h (143mph). The jaws open to 180° and close within 0.13 milliseconds. This rapidly shutting jaw can be used to grab prey. A soldier termite, for example, is stunned or squashed, and even a nasute termite, which produces a jet of noxious secretion from its nozzle-shaped head, is incapacitated before it has a chance to squirt, making this one of the few ant species that can prey on this type of termite. The jaws can also be used defensively. The ant can strike an attacker, simultaneously flinging itself 20–23cm (8–9in.) away or snap its jaws on the ground, propelling itself high into the air. It possesses the fastest known self-powered predatory strike and defensive move in the entire animal kingdom.

Candidates for the world's fastest flying insects depend on how the speed is measured. The black cutworm *Agrotis ipsilon* has been clocked with a ground speed of up to 113km/h (70mph), but riding the winds ahead of cold fronts helps it along. Its air speed is only 13km/h (8mph). The highest air speeds so far recorded include the desert locust at 33km/h (21mph) and the corn earworm moth *Helicoverpa zea* at 28km/h (17mph), although there is the claim that a male horsefly *Hybomitra hinei* chased after an air rifle pellet at an estimated speed of 143km/h (89mph).

The animal with the world's biggest testicles relative to its body size is the bush cricket *Platycleis affinis*. They represent 14 per cent of the insect's body mass, compared to 0.5 per cent in humans. However, these crickets don't release any more sperm than their less endowed relatives. Females of the species are ultra-promiscuous, so the males don't want to spend all their seed in one place.

BACK FROM THE BRINK

The Lord Howe tree lobster *Dryococelus australis* is one of the rarest insects in the world. It was thought to have become extinct due to rats infesting Lord Howe Island, off the coast of eastern Australia, but in 2001 a small population of about thirty was found under a single *Melaleuca howeana* shrub on Ball's Pyramid, south-east of Lord Howe, a stark rocky islet and the tallest volcanic stack in the world. The tree lobster is a flightless member of the stick insect family, but more closely resembles a cross between a grasshopper and a cockroach. It also had one more surprise for visiting researchers. DNA analysis revealed that the species evolved more than 20 million years ago, 13 million years before the rocks on Lord Howe Island were formed. It means it must have evolved on another island which is now submerged. Lord Howe Island is the youngest of a chain of volcanic islands that formed over a hotspot in the Earth's crust. As the continental plate on which it sat moved northwards, the island moved away from the hotspot and without molten rock being fed from below, the sea gradually eroded it until it became a submarine mount. The tree lobster must have migrated somehow to the younger islands before its original island disappeared.

THE WORLD'S SMALLEST ANIMALS

The world's smallest frogs were discovered in New Guinea in 2011. *Paedophryne dekot* and *P. verrucosa* are both just 8–9 mm (0.32–0.35in.) long. A pair of them could sit on a drawing pin.

The world's smallest bird is the bee hummingbird *Mellisuga helenae* from the island of Cuba. It is 50mm (2in.) long and weighs 1.8g (0.064oz).

The smallest bat is Kitti's hog-nosed or bumblebee bat *Craseonycteris thonglongyai* from the limestone caves of Thailand and Burma. It's about 30mm (1.2in.) long and weighs 2g (0.07oz), making it also the smallest mammal, although there are claims that Savi's pygmy shrew *Suncus etruscus* is smaller.

The world's smallest fish is the newly discovered (2006) *Paedocypris progenetica* from forest swamps in Sumatra. It's just 7.9mm (0.31in.) long, and has grasping fins. It lives in water with an acidity of pH 3, and its brain has no protective bone surrounding it.

The smallest snake is a newly discovered (2008) thread snake *Leptotyphlops carlae* from Barbados. It's as thin as spaghetti and 100mm (3.9in.) long.

A male fairyfly of the species *Dicopomorpha echmepterygis* from Costa Rica is the world's smallest insect. It is 0.139mm (0.005in.) long, smaller than a single-celled *Paramecium*. It's a type of wasp, but the male has no eyes, no wings, a simple hole for a mouth and the smallest known brain. At the ends of its legs are suction cups which attach to the female, which is much larger than the male.

The newly discovered (2001) jaragua sphaero or dwarf gecko *Sphaerodactylus ariasae,* from the island of Beata in the Dominican Republic, shares the title of world's smallest lizard with *S. parthenopion* from the British Virgin Islands. They are both about 16mm (0.63in.) long.

The smallest known chameleon is the minute leaf chameleon *Brookesia minima*. Males are 28mm (1.1in.) long – though the female is slightly larger – and they live on the forest floor of Nosy Be, an island off the north-east coast of Madagascar.

The world's smallest primate is Madame Berthe's mouse lemur *Microcebus berthae* from western Madagascar, with an average body length of 92mm (3.6in.) and weight of about 30g (1oz).

The world's smallest living crocodile is Cuvier's dwarf caiman *Paleosuchus palpebrosus from* South America. Females are about 1.2m (3.94ft) long and the males a little bigger.

The world's smallest echinoderm is a tiny sea cucumber *Psammothuria ganapatii*. It is only 4mm (0.16in.) long and lives amongst the sand grains on beaches on the Waltair coast of India.

MYSTERY SOLVED?

How did the zebra *Equus* get its stripes? It sounds like another of Rudyard Kipling's *Just So Stories,* but this story is not fanciful. The striped pattern disrupts the light patterns that insects, such as tsetse flies and horseflies (Family: Tabanidae) use to find food and water. Normally, horseflies and their relatives are attracted to dark-coloured animals because the darker colour reflects light waves polarised in the same direction, which is the same as those reflected from water where the flies lay their eggs. White coats do not reflect light in the same way and are less likely to attract flies. In tests of different colour patterns by evolutionary ecologists from Lund University, they found that striped patterns were even less attractive to the flies than the white surfaces. Stripes reflect multiple light patterns. They surmised that this could be a reason that the zebra is striped.

THE WORLD'S MOST MYSTERIOUS ANIMALS

The many diverse forms of the Y-larva, also known as facetotectans, are probably the most mysterious animals in the world. They were first discovered as long ago as 1899, and despite them being commonly occurring organisms in plankton and found through-out the world's oceans from the tropics to the poles, nobody has known what an adult Y-organism looks like or what it does. It is the only animal that is described from its larval stage alone. However, research at the University of Copenhagen is beginning to offer up some clues. Y-larvae start out in life as miniscule, free-swimming, shrimp-like creatures, so the researchers collected these in plankton nets and, in an aquarium, exposed them to hormones that encouraged them to mature. The result was quite a shock. The larvae shed their exoskeletons, lost their muscles, digestive tracts and eyes, and each of them turned into an amorphous, slug-like, pulsing mass of cells. The researchers called it an 'ypsigon' and its form suggested it to be a parasite – but the 100-year-old mystery is not over yet. They believe this stage is not the adult but a second larval stage. Which animal the ypsigon and its adult-form parasite turns into, is still unknown.

GETTING ABOUT

American lobsters *Homarus americanus* get about quickly on the seabed by 'jet-assisted walking'. On the underside of their abdomen are tiny paddles, known as pleopods, which are fanned rapidly to help push the animal forward. They deliver the same amount of thrust as the fins of a bluegill sunfish *Lepomis macro-chirus* or a surfperch *Embiotoca jacksoni*, which use their pectoral fins to swim at moderate speeds. The lobster's pleopods are, in effect, auxiliary thrusters which assist walking, especially over obstacles.

Sharks are highly efficient swimmers. Their skin is covered with tiny teeth (dermal denticles) that move and flex as the shark swims, channelling the water across the body in the most effective way. Vortices or eddies, which normally form close to the surface of a smooth body and slow down the animal, are kept away from the shark's body by the denticles. This reduces drag by as much as 8 per cent and helps the animal move 12.3 per cent faster, so the shark can swim further on any given amount of energy. The denticles on some species, such as the fast-swimming mako shark *Isurus*, are narrower at the bottom than at the top. They can be flexed to an angle of 60° or more – a process called 'denticle bristling' – so the shark positions its denticles to optimise its swimming speed and manoeuvrability. The shark's tail also gives the shark a boost. When you look at the water behind most fish, their tails produce a vortex at the end of each tail flick. It pushes the water aside and then sends it spiralling away when it changes direction. However, as the shark tail swings from side to side, observers see two vortices – a small vortex at the end of the stroke and a large one when the tail reaches the midline. It shows that the shark stiffens its tail for a second in mid-swing, delivering added thrust.

The American alligator *Alligator mississipiensis* can steer underwater by shifting air from air sacs on one side of the body to those on the other. Only part of the alligator's lung is used for breathing: the honeycombed portion transfers oxygen to and receives carbon dioxide from the muscles via the blood system. It breathes in and out using chest muscles, much like humans do. The rest of the lungs are divided into large flexible sacs that simply store air, and they are filled and emptied with a fan-shaped muscle – the diaphragmaticus – connecting the lungs with the pelvis. In tests at the University of Utah, it was found that the alligator switches on this muscle, along with three other breathing muscles, even when it is submerged and not breathing. It shifts air between the sacs to help it dive, rise to the surface and turn left and right. If the sacs are stretched towards the pelvis, for example, the rear of the body is more buoyant than the front, so the alligator can dive without causing a disturbance on the surface, a useful ability to have when stalking prey. Shifting air to one side or the other helps the body to roll and the animal to turn, again without stirring up the water – the ultimate stealth predator.

Lizards, such as the Florida scrub lizard *Sceloporus woodi*, are able to race away rapidly from a standing start by changing their first few strides, and the secret is all in the ankles and toes. The first stride is a jumping motion, very similar to the explosive jumps in frogs, and the second stride continues the acceleration. By the third stride, the lizard is running at top speed.

The sandfish *Scincus scincus* is a lizard that lives in the Sahara desert. It moves through the sand, not using its tiny legs but by holding its limbs flat to its sides and swimming with undulations of its body, like an eel.

Geckoes have microscopic branching hairs on their feet and they leave footprints. A fatty secretion of phospholipids protects the hairs. It might also provide the liquid layer that makes the toes stick better to flat surfaces, including glass, enabling the gecko to clamber around on vertical walls and even ceilings. Geckoes also climb better when it's humid. Humidity makes the tiny hairs on the bottom of their feet softer and stickier, enabling them to stick to walls like chewing gum. But if they encounter a slippery patch they immediately push their tails against the wall to ensure their front feet are planted firmly. And if they should fall, they can right themselves in a tenth of a second by snapping their tail so they land on all four feet.

By the laws of physics, enormous spiders as big as tarantulas shouldn't be able to climb smooth, vertical walls but they do, albeit with difficulty. Their secret is also on the bottom of their feet, which are covered with microscopic hairs. If they feel themselves falling, some of these hairs have extended nozzle-like 'spigots' that secrete minute filaments of silk from their feet. They enable the spider to hold on. Spiders known to have this capability include the Chilean rose *Grammostola rosea*, the Indian ornametal *Poecilotheria regalis* and the Mexican flame knee *Brachypelma auratum*, but it's likely that all tarantulas have the capability.

Orangutans *Pongo* have green credentials. They use 30 per cent less energy than would be expected for their size. It means an orangutan moving through the trees burns fewer calories than a person sitting in front of the television. In the wild, it means that these apes can better survive in lean times.

ANIMAL ATHLETES

Under research conditions, the cheetah *Acinonyx jubatus* has been clocked at 113km/h (70mph) in short bursts of 200m (about 200 yards). It is the supreme sprinter and the world's fastest mammal. Unlike other cats, it has feet with permanently extended claws, like running spikes, and an ultra-flexible spine that enables the animal to stretch its body on every stride.

North America's pronghorn antelope *Antilocapra americana* is a long-distance runner. It is not a true antelope, but fills the same niche; a case of convergent evolution. Its top speed is in the region of 100km/h (60mph), making it the fastest mammal in North America and the second fastest on the planet, after the cheetah. However, unlike the cheetah, it can keep going at speed for long periods, an ability it evolved to outrun the now extinct North American cheetah *Myracinonyx trumani*.

African hunting dogs *Lycaon pictus* are the relay winners. They wear down their prey. First one pair of dogs in the pack will harry the target, racing along at up to 56km/h (35mph), and when they tire two or three more will take over. The victim has little hope of escaping. The dogs, which have four toes on each foot rather than the usual five, are so adept at long-distance pursuit that they achieve a kill on nine out of ten hunts, compared to a lion pride which is successful only 30 per cent of the time.

The spittlebug or froghopper *Philaenus spumarius* is the best high jumper. Research at Cambridge University has shown that it leaps 70cm (28in.) high, even though the little creature is no more than 6mm (0.2in.) long. It's the insect equivalent of us leaping over a tall building. It experiences an acceleration of 400 G (G-force), relying on the use of stored energy like a catapult. The legs are held in a cocked position, the two main leg muscles building energy until it's released, and the froghopper whizzes off at 4m per second (13ft/sec.).

The same Cambridge team observed the hedgehog flea *Archaeopsyllus erinacei*, the world champion long-jumper. It can jump 200 times its own body length, about 33cm (13in.). Prior to jumping, energy is stored in a kind of internal 'coiled spring' of resilin, in the thorax rather than in the muscles, and a system of multi-jointed levers in the rear legs enables the animal to drive its tarsus (toe) into the ground at takeoff. Large spines help it grip the ground.

The common basilisk *Basiliscus basiliscus* of Latin America can move its legs so fast that it can actually run a short distance across the surface of water, which gave rise to its nickname, the Jesus Christ lizard. It has large hind feet with scaly fringes on three of the toes that, when they hit water, increase the surface area of the foot. The first slap on the surface pushes water away and creates pockets of air underneath. The lizard then thrusts forward, followed by a recovery stroke and a repeat of the process. Young lizards can run up to 20m (65ft) without sinking, but older basilisks are not quite so nimble.

Another great jumper is the frog, but a frog's leap is theoretically impossible. The distance covered – up to five times its body length – requires more power than its muscles should have. The frog achieves this by becoming a living catapult. The leg muscles contract long before the frog leaps. This loads energy into its ankle tendon which, when released, enables the frog to travel much further than if it was using its muscles alone. Champion jumper is Australia's 5cm (2in.) long rocket frog *Litoria nasuta* with a leap of 2m (6.6ft).

The hop, skip and jump champion must be the flying fish. There are two types of 'wing' configuration: *Exocoetus* has one pair of wings, while *Cypselurus* has two pairs. The wings are actually modified fins, and in cross-section they're curved like a bird's wing to maximise lift. The fish can leave the water at high speed – up to 70km/h (43mph). It moves its tail seventy times per second, spreads its wings and tilts them upwards to provide lift. A typical glide might be 50m (160ft), but if the fish wants to continue it drops to the water, rapidly wags its tail on the surface and propels itself even further. Using the updraughts of air at the leading edge of waves it can fly up to 6m (20ft) above the sea's surface and cover a distance of 400m (1,300ft). It uses this flying ability to escape fast-swimming predators (see below). Sometimes flying fish land on the decks of ships; in May 2008, a flying fish was filmed off Yakushima Island, Japan, which flew for forty-five seconds, beating the previous record, held since 1920, by three seconds.

Not surprisingly, fish win top swimming honours. The estimated speed of the 3m (9.8ft) long sailfish *Istiophorus* is 109km/h (68mph), when leaping, making it the fastest fish in the sea. Close behind is its billfish relative, the 4.2m (13.8ft) long striped marlin *Tetrapturus audax* with a top speed of 80km/h

(50mph), along with the yahoo *Acanthocybium solandri* at 78km/h (48mph), the 2.8m (8.2ft) long southern bluefin tuna *Thunnus maccoyii* at 76km/h (47mph) and the smaller yellowfin tuna *Thunnus albacares* at 74km/h (46mph).

Two species of sharks are on the fast-swimming podium. The shortfin mako shark *Isurus oxyrinchus* has been clocked at 74km/h (46mph) in a short burst (not leaping like the billfish), and the 3.8m (13ft) long blue shark *Prionace glauca* is capable of a short burst at 69km/h (43mph).

Whales are not usually noted for their speed, but the 27m (88.5ft) long fin whale *Balaenoptera physalus* is not only the world's second largest animal, but is also known as the 'greyhound of the seas'. It cruises at speeds up to 37km/h (23mph), which is quite a turn of speed when its size is considered and that it is trying to plough through a dense medium like water. It can accelerate to bursts of up to 48km/h (30mph).

The world's largest dolphin – the 7m (23ft) long orca or killer whale *Orcinus orca* – is able to reach speeds in excess of 56km/h (34.5mph), making it one of the world's fastest marine mammals. Other dolphins can also power through the water. A spotted dolphin *Stenella* was clocked at 40km/h (24.7mph) in a sprint and a speedy Dall's porpoise *Phocoenoides dalli* has been recorded at 56km/h (34.5mph), making it equal champion with the killer whale, which it frequently has to escape.

DEEPEST DIVERS

During 2003 and 2004, researchers from the Woods Hole Oceanographic Institute and other European institutions tagged Cuvier's beaked whales *Ziphius cavirostris* in the Ligurian Sea off Italy. The whales dived to a maximum depth of 1,900m (6,234ft) with a maximum dive duration of eighty-five minutes. Their average dive depth was 1,070m (3,510ft) and average duration fifty-eight minutes. They also tagged Blainville's beaked whales *Mesoplodon densirostris* swimming in deep water off the Canary Islands. They were found to dive to 1,250m (4,101ft) for fifty-seven minutes, and had an average dive depth of 835m (2,740ft) with an average duration of 46.5 minutes. Between long, deep dives, during which the whales were probably hunting for food, both species undertook a series of shallow dives to rest near the surface. This would mean they are amongst the world's deepest diving air-breathing animals.

The sperm whale *Physeter macrocephalus* dives for up to an hour to more than 1,200m (3,937ft), with average dives of forty-five minutes to depths of 400–600m (1,312–1,969ft). Down there it tackles such monsters as giant *Architeuthis* and colossal squid *Mesonychoteuthis hamiltoni*. One of the deepest known sperm whale dives was a whale that dived down to the bottom of the ocean and became entangled in a deep-sea cable lying 1,135m (3,724ft) below the surface, but there are claims for dives down to 2,000m (6,562ft).

The northern elephant seal *Mirounga angustirostris* has been known to dive down to 1,500m (4,921ft) for two hours, although average dives are to 350–700m (1,148–2,297ft) for twenty-five to thirty minutes, and a southern elephant seal *Mirounga leonina* has been tracked to 1,200m (3,937ft). Weddell seals *Leptonychotes weddellii* go down to 700m (2,297ft), and might dive continuously for eleven hours, but they have to rest and recuperate afterwards for at least thirteen hours.

A northern bottlenose whale *Hyperoodon ampulla-tus*, tagged by researchers from Canada's Dalhousie University, reached a depth of 1,453m (4,767ft) during a seventy-minute dive, and other individuals dived regularly beyond 800m (2,625ft). Narwhals *Monodon monoceros* occasionally dive to depths greater than 1,000m (3,281ft), as do leatherback turtles *Dermochelys coriacea*, the deepest diving reptile. They have been tracked to 1,250m (4,101ft), remaining at this depth for more than an hour.

The emperor penguin *Aptenodytes forsteri* is the deepest diving bird. It dives to 535m (1,755ft), remaining below for up to eighteen minutes while hunting for fish and squid, but how does it know when it's time to surface? It seems they don't monitor elapsed time, but respond to the cumulative work of their swimming muscles. On average birds remain below for 287 wing flaps.

Even the diminutive little or fairy penguin *Eudyptula minor* of Australasian waters can dive unexpectedly deep. In November 2005, such a penguin, tagged by researchers from Tokyo's National Institute of Polar Research, was swimming off Philip Island when it dived and reached a depth of 66.7m (219ft), the maximum theoretical depth for a penguin of its size, and it stayed down for ninety seconds. Its flock mates rarely went below 50m (164ft). Similarly a Peruvian diving petrel *Pelecanoides garnotii* reached 83.1m (273ft), even though theoretically a seabird of this size should be able to go only to 46m (151ft).

EPIC JOURNEYS

The world's greatest traveller is the Arctic tern *Sterna paradisaea*. In 2009, individuals fitted with GPS tracking devices by the Greenland Institute of Natural Resources were found to have followed a zigzag course across the Atlantic Ocean on their migration between Greenland and the Antarctic. On their way south they stop off in the North Atlantic, at the front between cold productive northern waters and warmer less productive southern waters, for twenty-five days to fuel up before travelling down the Brazilian or West African coast. The return journey north follows an S-shaped path up the middle of the Atlantic. It was found that birds are making round trips each year of 71,000km (44,000 miles), beating their nearest rival – sooty shearwaters *Puffinus griseus*, which make a figure-of-eight migration of about 65,000km (39,000 miles) around the Pacific Ocean, as revealed in similar research by University of California at Santa Cruz biologists. The terns' zigzag flight plan, like the shearwaters', follows the prevailing winds at different latitudes, so they rarely fly into a strong headwind. Some terns live to a grand old age of thirty years, and they will have flown a staggering 2.4 million kilometres (1.5 million miles) or three excursions to the Moon and back during their lifetime. Each year, they undertake the longest migration of any animal on the planet and in doing so fly to where the sun never sets.

Humpback whales *Megaptera novaeangliae* are world travellers, too. They migrate between tropical waters where they breed to temperate and polar seas where they feed. Most remain in one hemisphere, and never meet whales from the other hemisphere, but there is one population in the eastern Pacific that breaks all the rules. During the southern spring, the whales migrate northwards along the west coast of South America in the cold Humboldt current. The current flows all the way to the Galapagos Islands on the Equator, so in order to find warm waters suitable for calving they must travel across the Equator and into the northern hemisphere. They prefer water with a temperature of 21–28°C (70–82°F), which they find off Costa Rica. Whales from a northern hemisphere population also travel to Costa Rica from California, and some remain all year round so here, and only here, could north and south humpbacks meet. The southern hemisphere whales journey from the Antarctic, a distance of at least 8,510km (5,288 miles), the longest migration undertaken by any mammal on Earth.

On 9 May 2010, a grey whale *Eschrichtius robustus* was spotted off the coast of Israel, and twenty-three days later it was seen again off Barcelona, about 3,000km (1,865 miles) away. They might seem unremarkable observations until you realise that the species has been extinct in the northern Atlantic Ocean since the seventeenth or eighteenth century on the American side and since 500AD on the European side, probably due to overhunting. Today, grey whales embark on great journeys along the coasts bordering the north-west and north-east Pacific. On the American side, for example, the whales travel the 11,000km (6,800 miles) between Baja California, where they breed, to the Bering and Chukchi seas where they feed. Where the Mediterranean whale came from and where it was heading is a mystery, although speculation is that it might have travelled from the Pacific (where it could have been a member of the north-east Pacific population) to the Atlantic, because northern routes between the oceans are becoming increasingly ice-free due to global warming.

A male southern elephant seal *Mirounga leonina*, nicknamed Jackson, was satellite-tagged on a beach in Tierra del Fuego and then followed for the next year, during which he meandered northwards in and out of fjords along the Chilean coast and ventured out and over the continental shelf into deep water in the Pacific Ocean. In less than twelve months, he travelled almost 29,000km (18,000 miles), the equivalent of a journey from New York to Sydney and back again.

Great white sharks *Carcharodon carcharias* were once thought to be stay-at-home predators, but now we know differently. In November 2003, a tagged female shark at Dyer Island, South Africa, headed out across the Indian Ocean and turned up ninety-nine days later, in February 2004, near Exmouth, Western Australia. Her distinctive dorsal fin was then spotted in August 2004, back in South Africa. She had made a round trip of about 20,000km (12,000 miles) in about nine months. And the Indian Ocean great whites are not the only travelling population. In the Pacific Ocean, Californian great whites migrate to an area between Baja California and Hawaii known to researchers as 'White Shark Café'. They travel slowly, diving frequently to 900m (3,000ft), but when they arrive they start to make short dives to 300m (1,000ft). They hang around at the café for about a hundred days, some sharks going on to Hawaii, before returning again to California. Why they go and what they do there is still a complete mystery.

Common eels *Anguilla anguilla* have an extraordinary life cycle. They hatch from eggs in the Sargasso Sea, to the east of the Bahamas, and as a transparent leptocephalus larvae, they travel in the ocean currents, such as the Gulf Stream and North Atlantic Drift – part of the North Atlantic Gyre – towards Europe. They ascend rivers as glass eels, swimming against the current, to places where they'll grow into eels that can be a metre (about 3ft) long. When mature, they swim back down the rivers and out into the Atlantic Ocean, returning to the Sargasso Sea to spawn. What route they take on their 5,000km (3,000-mile) return journey has been a mystery; that is, until scientists from Britain, Denmark, Norway, Ireland and Canada placed pop-up satellite tags on twenty-two adult silver eels and released them off the coast of Galway in western Ireland. So far, the research has revealed how the eels behave during the first 1,300km (800 miles) of their journey. They do not swim directly across the Atlantic in a straight line, but they rejoin the North Atlantic Gyre, following the Canary Current to the west of Africa where they probably follow the North Equatorial Current back to the Sargasso. At night they swim close to the surface, while during the day they dive to a maximum depth of 1,000m (3,280ft). Chasing prey is unlikely to be a reason, for they appear not to feed during their migration; it's possible that this strategy helps them avoid predators. In addition, swimming in the warmer surface waters enables them to maintain a high metabolism and optimise swimming activity during the day, while the cooler waters help delay gonad development until they reach their destination, especially important when they enter the sub-tropical currents in the latter stages of their migration. Now the researchers are hoping to fill in the rest of the journey.

Leatherback turtles *Dermochelys coriacea* travel great distances and sometimes reach great depths. At over 2m (6.6ft) long, it is the largest of the marine turtles and one of the few reptiles that can maintain a high body temperature, up to 18°C (32.4°F) above the temperature of the surrounding seawater, enabling it to dive to 1,280m (4,200ft) deep and stay down for up to seventy minutes – although generally dives tend to be little more than five minutes. Female sea turtles nesting in Suriname might travel across the North Atlantic to feed on the abundance of jellyfish off the west coast of Scotland, while in the Pacific, females nesting on Costa Rica's beaches travel a narrow corridor past the Galapagos Islands, across the Equator and into the South Pacific Gyre. One individual, tagged at a nesting beach in the Papua province of Indonesia, journeyed first to Oregon before heading for Hawaii, when the batteries of its satellite transmitter ran out. It had travelled 20,558km (12,774 miles) in 647 days and was still going strong, making it another contender for the most travelled vertebrate on Earth.

Saltwater crocodiles *Crocodylus porosus* occasionally leave their home rivers and ride the ocean currents to distant lands. There are many old seadog tales of large crocodiles spotted far out at sea, but it was not until researchers from the University of Queensland tracked crocodiles along Australia's north-east coast that it was found that sometimes they do head out to sea, but only when the currents are favourable. Many simply travelled the 48km (30 miles) or so to the river mouth, but some go beyond, always leaving within an hour of the tide changing. One individual – a 3.84m (12.6ft) long male – left the Kennedy River and journeyed 590km (366 miles) over twenty-five days to reach the Gulf of Carpentaria in time for the start of a seasonal current system. A larger 4.84m (15.8ft) male travelled 411km (255 miles) through the Torres Straits. When the animal arrived the current was running opposite to his direction of travel, so he waited in a sheltered bay for four days until it reversed. It's not clear why these crocs make such journeys, but they do tend to congregate at places with seasonally abundant fish, such as the Mary River. On one occasion, forty enormous beasts were seen feeding together there. Their prey was migrating mullet which swim upriver on the rising tide to breed. The research also goes some way to explaining how these animals reach remote islands right across the Indo-Pacific region, from India in the west as far as Fiji in the east.

How migrating birds find their way is still much of a mystery, but slowly pieces of evidence are slotting into place. The sun, stars and the Earth's magnetic field have all been implicated in bird navigation; in fact, recent research has revealed that a bird 'sees' its magnetic flight plan, for a molecule that senses magnetism exists in a bird's eye. For domestic pigeons *Columba livia f. domestica*, at least, familiar landmarks also play an important role. Researchers at the University of Zurich have been able to monitor the brain waves of flying pigeons and they found that high-frequency brain waves became more intense when a bird passed a familiar landmark. The results showed that the birds had recognised the sites they had visited before. Whether this is an important navigational cue or simply a case of object recognition has yet to be established. In another study in Pisa, pigeons with their right nostril blocked had more difficulty finding their home, so the sense of smell might also be involved.

Long-haul birds need water on their epic journeys, but to avoid stopping too often they find it internally. They burn muscle, even though they have sufficient fat stores on board. A possible reason is that this yields five times as much water per unit of energy as burning fat. The birds burn muscle protein to keep hydrated and this varies depending on the humidity of the air that they are flying through.

Birds use performance-enhancing drugs. The semi-palmated sandpiper *Calidris pusilla* is a long-distance migrant which sets out each autumn from its summer breeding grounds in the Canadian Arctic and travels south at about 60km/h (37mph) for more than 3,000km (1,864 miles) to South America. Part of the journey is a gruelling three-day flight over open water and only the fittest birds make it. They prepare well. The shortening days and general drop in temperature trigger hormonal changes that cause the bird's gut to enlarge and its diet to change so it puts on more weight. It exercises more frequently, building up its flight muscles so it's ready for the marathon journey. The surprise comes early in the flight. It puts down on the shores of the Bay of Fundy, where the biggest tides in the world occur, and sets about eating mud shrimps *Corophium volutator*, 5mm (0.2in.) long amphipod crustaceans that are packed with exceptionally high levels of omega-3 fatty acids. Over the next couple of weeks, the bird consumes up to 23,000 shrimps on each tide and its body weight doubles; but that's not all: the fatty acids boost the oxygen uptake in its flight muscles, priming them for endurance exercise, i.e. doping to improve muscle performance! The effect is greater than ten weeks' endurance training for a horse and seven weeks for a human. It ensures the strongest birds make it all the way to their winter home in Suriname.

Small birds, such as the Swainson's thrush *Catharus ustulatus*, migrate at night to avoid predators and to take advantage of the calmer conditions usually experienced at night. If they come to large natural barriers, such as the Gulf of Mexico, they might have to travel non-stop for twenty-four hours, so when they do eventually put down they must be pretty tired. They sleep during the day, but to stay alert they only sleep with one eye closed and one half of the brain asleep at any one time. The other half remains awake and the other eye open so the bird is ready to react to any disturbance. Marine mammals, such as dolphins and whales, adopt the same system.

Northern wheatears *Oenanthe oenanthe* are marathon flyers. In summer, they nest across Eurasia,

Canada and Alaska, but come the winter they head south. Birds from eastern Canada cross to Greenland and then south-east to western Africa, but the Alaskan birds embark on even greater journeys. They head out across Russia, then down through the Arabian Peninsula to Kenya – and they don't hang about. They complete their 14,500km (9,000-mile) journey in just ninety days.

Falcons were not thought to spend extended periods at sea, but now researchers from Oxford University tagging birds in Greenland have found that the gyr falcon *Falco rusticolus* is an exception: it's a secret seabird. During the winter, it swoops over ice floes and packs of ice, hunting seabirds such as black guillemots *Cepphus grylle*, using icebergs as lookout points. And the area of the High Arctic over which these birds fly is enormous: falcons on the west coast of Greenland cover up to 6,657 sq. km (2,570 sq. miles) and those on the east coast up to 63,647 sq. km (24,574 sq. miles), some spending as many as forty consecutive days at sea, resting on the sea ice. One female in the study travelled 4,548km (2.826 miles) over 200 days, half of that time over the sea between Greenland and Iceland. This ability to travel great distances and exploit scattered sources of food has enabled the gyr falcon to survive in one of the most inhospitable places on Earth.

The wandering albatross *Diomedea exulans* travels enormous distances in order to collect food for its offspring. One bird was reliably recorded on a 6,000km (3,730-mile) journey that took twelve days, and many are thought to journey even further. Outside the breeding season birds may circumnavigate Antarctica, carried by the prevailing winds in the Southern Ocean. With the longest wings of any bird, it soars like a glider, using the updraughts that rise at the front of ocean waves. It only lands on the sea's surface at night to feed on squid and fish or to roost, but it will follow fishing boats for scraps and will steal from long lines. Many are hooked and killed. However, the albatross is one species that seems to benefit, albeit briefly, from climate changes. During the past fifty years, the westerly winds in the Southern Ocean have speeded up and shifted southwards towards Antarctica, enabling the birds to fly faster, shorten their foraging trips, and feed closer to the sub-Antarctic islands on which they breed. The result is fitter parents bringing up healthier broods.

Young wandering albatrosses *Diomedea exulans* are equally accomplished travellers, according to work by French and Swedish researchers in the Crozet and Kergulen islands in the southern Indian Ocean. One particular juvenile female albatross left her nest site and the island for eight days, during which she practised flying but was not feeding so she lost a kilogram (2.2lb) in weight. She remained in the vicinity for another nine days, before heading north-east on southerly tailwinds. During the next seven months she covered 52,346km (32,526 miles), travelling on average 610km (380 miles) per day, which meant she probably flew the equivalent of 4.6 times around the Earth during her first year of life; this would have been alone and without any assistance from her parents. She was then expected to spend another four or five years at sea, before returning briefly to her natal nest site, where one day she will nurture one of the next generation of ocean travellers.

Black-browed albatrosses *Thalassarche melanophrys* also scour the Southern Ocean for widely scattered food, but they have a way to increase their chances of finding it: they feed alongside killer whales *Orcinus orca*. The killer whales chase fish and squid towards the surface where the albatrosses can pick them off with ease. Tropical seabirds show similar associations with shoals of tuna.

Each autumn hundreds of millions of monarch butterflies *Danaus plexippus* migrate across North America, setting out from as far north as eastern Canada and heading for the forests of central Mexico to spend the winter. They navigate by the sun, but somehow they must appreciate that it moves across the sky during the course of the day. It was once thought that the biological clock, with which the insect can adjust its calculations as the day passes, was in the butterfly's brain, but research at the University of Massachusetts Medical School has revealed that the clock is in its antennae. Even so, researchers still don't know for sure how the butterfly knows which way to go in the first place, although cryptochrome, one of the light-sensitive proteins found in the monarch butterfly's antennae clock, acts as a magnetic field sensor in fruit flies, so the Earth's magnetic field could well help the butterflies set off in the right direction.

Globe skimmer dragonflies *Pantala flavescens* and a few related species could well oust the monarch butterfly from the world's top insect migration slot. They travel from southern India to East Africa via the Maldives and back again. They fly, glide and soar at altitudes up to 1,000m (3,280ft), and follow weather systems with favourable hind winds, crossing 3,500km (2,175 miles) of open ocean during one leg of the journey. Several bird species embark on a similar journey, many of which eat dragonflies.

RECORD-BREAKING BIRDS

The fastest bird in the skies is undoubtedly the peregrine falcon *Falco peregrinus* during its hunting stoop. It first climbs high above its prey and then folds its wings and hurtles down like an aerial torpedo. Specially designed nostrils, like the intake ramps and inlet cones of jet engines, slow the intake of air, otherwise the air pressure would damage the bird's lungs. A third eyelid – the nictitating membrane – protects the eye and spreads tears to clear it of any dust or debris. It slams into the wing of its target with its foot, tightened like a clenched fist, to prevent the prey from flying away, and then turns and grabs its prize, flying at a more leisurely pace to a perch or the ground to eat its meal. In an experiment in 2005, US falconer Ken Franklin had one of his birds clocked accurately at a top speed of 389km/h (242 mph). This means the peregrine is the world's fastest moving animal.

The world's highest-flying bird in powered flight is the bar-headed goose *Anser indicus*. On its annual migration flights between breeding grounds in Central Asia and wintering sites in northern India, Pakistan and Burma, it flies over the Himalayas, almost as high as Everest. According to Bangor University biologist Lucy Hawkes, birds were observed at 6,437m (21,120ft), and it's likely they fly even higher. They can achieve this by breathing in and out very rapidly, having blood with a greater affinity for oxygen and having a greater number of capillaries to deliver it to the muscles. The muscles themselves have more mitochondria to release more energy quickly.

Other high-flyers include a mallard duck *Anas platy-rhynchos* that on 9 July 1962 collided with an aircraft at 6,400m (21,000ft) between Battle Mountain and Elko, Nevada; and whooper swans that have been seen by pilots at about 8,230m (27,000ft) over the Atlantic between Iceland and Scotland in recent years.

In 1921, bearded vultures or lammergeiers *Gypaetus barbatus* were seen by an Everest climbing expedition at not less than 7,620m (25,000ft), according to one of the climbers. On the same expedition ravens

Corvus corax, red-billed choughs *Pyrrhocorax pyrrhocorax,* alpine choughs *Pyrrhocorax graculus* and black-eared kites *Milvus lineatus* were seen from their camp at 6,096m (20,000ft) and they even saw a hoopoe *Upupa epops* flying over the Karta glacier at 6,400m (21,000ft). In a 1924 expedition ravens were seen at 6,350m (20,600ft), and on other occasions red-billed choughs have been spotted at 7,950m (26,080ft) on Everest, and alpine choughs at 8,200m (26,900ft).

The highest known bird that soars, rather than using powered flight, is Rüppell's griffon vulture *Gyps rueppellii.* On 29 November 1973, one vulture was sucked into the jet engine of a commercial aircraft flying over Abidjan, Côte d'Ivoire, at an altitude of about 11,278m (37,000ft). To reach such lofty heights, the vulture uses thermals of rising hot air, like a lift, to spiral slowly upwards and then glides down gradually at an angle, only to pick up the next thermal and do it all over again. In this way, it gains a free ride to wherever it wants to go.

FLIGHT DETAILS

Aircraft have Pitot tubes (invented by French engineer Henri Pitot) on their wings that detect airflow. They're speedometers for aircraft that indicate to a pilot, amongst other things, whether he's likely to stall. Now, researchers at the University of Maryland have found similar devices on the wings of bats. Tiny hairs set on domes of sensory cells are dotted around the bat's wing membranes, sending signals to the bat's brain about airflow over and around the wing. It's this that probably helps the animal to fly effectively and efficiently.

Swifts *Apus apus,* like most birds, change the shape of their wings to maximise their flying capability when undertaking different tasks. When chasing after insects, the wings are swept back, as much as 50°, giving speed and manoeuvrability and tripling their turn rate, but when sleeping on the wing, the wings are held out straight to double their glide time.

Eurasian chukar chicks do not fly over objects in their path but run over them while flapping their wings – so-called 'flap-running'. Similarly, adult chukar partridges *Alectoris chukar* flap their wings to run up steep slopes and cliffs. In experiments, researchers at the University of Montana discovered that the birds use less than 10 per cent of the energy they would need to fly at the same angle, and they increase their flight muscle power by relatively small increments as the angle of the slope gradually increases. It means that flap-running by chicks, first up and over gentle inclines and then up and down steeper slopes, could be one way chukar chicks learn to fly, enabling them to build up their flight muscles gradually until it's time for their first proper flight. It also has implications for the origins of bird flight. At some point in the past, the small arms of bipedal dinosaurs evolved into wings, but the flight muscles of these creatures appear to be insufficient for powered flight. It is conceivable that they were used to flap-run up slopes and over obstacles, a precursor to true flight.

Landing is the riskiest part of flight. Hit the ground too fast and you crash; fly too slow and you stall, but insects get it just about right. Flies land on the ceiling by stretching out their front legs and grabbing hold, while their forward momentum swings their body round in a somersault until their remaining legs make contact. Honeybees *Apis mellifera*, however, are a little more dignified. As a bee approaches its landing site, it monitors the speed of images crossing its eyes to know its speed and slows dramatically until about 16mm away, where it hovers for 50–140 milliseconds. If the surface is horizontal, the rear pair of legs drops down to grab hold, before lowering the rest of the body. If the surface is vertical or overhead, like a ceiling, the bee checks the landing site with its antennae and then grabs with its front legs and hauls up its other two pairs of legs. The researchers who carried out the work at the University of Queensland discovered the bee's optimum landing site is a surface inclined at 60° to the horizontal. When flying fast its abdomen is held horizontally, but when it slows to land the abdomen drops, so the tips of the antenna and legs are in a plane of 60°, so antenna and legs touch down simultaneously. Now they want to find out if this angle is significant and whether the flowers that bees visit have the same natural tilt.

Emperor penguins *Aptenodytes forsteri* can fly, albeit no more than 45cm (18in.) above the sea's surface and very briefly. They fly because it's the only way to get back on the sea ice, and they achieve their short flight with the help of bubbles. The emperor has considerable control of its plumage, so, before it dives in, it raises its feathers to trap air underneath them. The air compresses as it dives deeper, shrinking as much as 75 per cent at a depth of 20m (65ft). The bird then depresses its feathers, locking the reduced air underneath. When it's time to return to the surface, the bird hurtles upwards and the expanding air pours through the feathers and coats the outside of its body, acting like a lubricant to reduce drag. As the bird rises, a trail of bubbles is left in its wake. In this way the emperor penguin rockets to the surface, reaching speeds of about 20km/h (12mph), enough momentum to see it airborne momentarily and safely onto the ice, where it lands on its chest.

MAGNETIC SENSE

A herd of domestic cattle or wild deer tends to stand or graze all with their heads facing either towards magnetic north or south. In the northern hemisphere, for example, red deer *Cervus eleaphus* and roe deer *Capreolus capreolus* all face north. The observations, made by German and Czech researchers while viewing herds in the field and on Google Earth, indicate that a magnetic sense is more widespread in animals and not confined to those that travel great distances. Red foxes *Vulpes vulpes* in the Czech Republic, for example, jump in any direction onto prey that they can clearly see, but they always jump on hidden prey in a north-easterly direction. It is thought the fox is using the Earth's magnetic field as a way to judge distances, for foxes tend to be more successful when hunting if they always jump the same distance. It might work like this: the fox 'sees' the ring of shadow on its retina which is darkest towards magnetic north and just like a normal shadow from a light source that follows you, it's always the same distance ahead. When stalking its prey, the fox edges forward towards the place where the sounds of its prey is coming from until the magnetic shadow lines up with it, at which point the fox is the critical distance away. Then, it pounces, and is 75 per cent successful when leaping towards the north-east.

American alligators *Alligator mississippiensis* and other crocodiles appear to use the Earth's magnetic field for navigation, and the Florida Fish and Wildlife Conservation Commission has put this knowledge to good use. Generally, when a 'nuisance' alligator is taken from an urban area and relocated deeper into the swamps, it will find its way back 'home', travelling at about 16km (10 miles) a week. However, if magnets are taped on either side of the alligator's head, it cannot find its way back – it's lost, so it stays put and becomes less of a threat to people.

PURE WHITE

Most American black bears are uniformly black, but on the west coast of Canada, black bears are white. These are the kermode bears *Ursus americanus kermodei* who live on Gribbell Island and Princess Royal Island where, isolated from predators, such as wolves and grizzly bears, they flourish alongside normal-coloured black bears, about 20–30 per cent of the total bear population. But, rather than stand out, these bears have a natural advantage over their black cousins. When they go fishing during the day, they are less visible to salmon and are 30 per cent more successful at making a catch. This means they fatten up in autumn when the salmon run, are better prepared for winter and more successful in rearing young. However, with salmon in decline, these special white black bears have an uncertain future.

Fifteen white saltwater crocodiles *Crocodylus porosus* live in Bhitarkanika National Park in Orissa, India. When they first hatched, they were yellowish with black markings, like most crocodiles, but later the yellowish colour faded to white. Two more white crocs were born at the Bhagabatpur crocodile-breeding park in the Sundarban Biosphere Reserve.

Nowadays, most – if not all – white tigers are in captivity. None has been reported from the wild for over fifty years. During the first half of the twentieth century, they were to be found in the forests of Bandhavgarh in India. Documents from the Rewa Palace indicate they had been seen on eight occasions. An orphaned white tiger was taken in by the Maharaja of Rewa, from which many other white tigers were bred and sent to zoos and circuses all over the world. They are not albinos, but colour mutants of the Royal Bengal tiger *Panthera tigris tigris*. They have white fur, black stripes and blue eyes.

Two prides of white lions have been reintroduced to their natural environment in Timbavita in northeast South Africa, close to the Kruger National Park. They are a rare colour mutation of the Kruger subspecies of African lion *Panthera leo krugeri*, which was first reported in 1928. Their blond to chalky white colour appears not to be a disadvantage, for the reintroduced lions are breeding and hunting in the wild without human intervention.

There are thought to be ten to fifteen pure white humpback whales *Megaptera novaeangliae* in the 15,000-strong population that visits Australia's Queensland coast each year. One of them is *Migaloo*, aboriginal for 'white fella', who was first seen as a calf in 1991. Another newborn calf was spotted near the Great Barrier Reef's Whitsunday Islands in September 2011. And, in 2008, a white southern right whale *Eubalaena australis* calf was spotted in Flinder's Bay in Western Australia.

Pure white Eurasian blackbirds *Turdus merula* appear from time to time. Just such a bird has been living in Rufford Abbey Country Park in Nottinghamshire, England. At one time it was not pure white, but due to a genetic mutation that prevents pigment from being deposited in its feathers, at each moult white feathers have replaced its black ones. By the summer of 2011, the bird was completely white.

On Aitcho Island in the South Shetlands, an all-white penguin breaks the uniform sea of black and white in a colony of chinstrap penguins *Pygoscelis antarcticus*. Tourists on a National Geographic Explorer expedition spotted the bird during the 2011–12 Antarctic summer.

In 2008, a white southern elephant seal *Mirounga leonina* was seen at Whale Bird Beach on Marion Island in the southern Indian Ocean, and in 2007 a white South American sea lion *Otaria flavescens* appeared at the Paso Shag narrows, near the Magellan Straits, Chile.

In December 2011, Project Toninhas biologists from Univille University spotted an albino toninha or La Plata dolphin *Pontoporia blainvillei* in the Bay of Babitonga in southern Brazil. This species is one of the river dolphins, but it tends to live in estuaries and sheltered inshore waters, rather than in freshwater. It has the longest beak for its body size of any cetacean.

Near the Commander Islands in the northern Pacific, Russian scientists are tracking a pure white killer whale *Orcinus orca* they've named Iceberg. First spotted in 2010, the whale is a large bull, thought to be about sixteen years old and described as 'breathtakingly beautiful'. Two smaller juvenile white orcas are known to live in the same area. A white orca is also plying the waters near the Kanaga volcano in the Aleutian Islands.

INDIVIDUALS

Sea anemones have personalities. Observing bead-let anemones *Actinia equina*, researchers from the University of Plymouth found that after they surprised the anemones with squirts of water, individuals would maintain their startle response for consistently the same amount of time. Some withdrew their tentacles for as little as three minutes, while others waited for up to twenty minutes before re-emerging. This makes the sea anemone the simplest animal thought to have a personality, joining a 'personality club' which includes octopuses and spiders.

Honeybees *Apis mellifera* are not as highly regimented as was first thought. Individuals that go scouting for a new nest site are more than three times as likely to be the same bees that seek out new food sources, bees that are willing to 'go the extra mile'. In humans this novelty-seeking behaviour is a component of personality, so bees, it seems, have personalities too.

LEFT- AND RIGHT-HANDED

Like us, most individual parrots are either left or right 'handed'. Researchers from Macquarie University observed many different species of Australian parrots. They found that because a parrot has its eyes on the side of its head it must cock its head one way or the other when looking to see what it's grasping with its foot. If the parrot grasps something with its right foot, it cocks its head to the left so its right eye can see better. At first, young parrots experiment by picking up food with either foot, but gradually form a preference for one. All individuals in four of the sixteen species observed possessed the same handedness. The researchers have never encountered a right-handed sulphur cockatoo *Cacatua galerita*, for example. Only one species showed no signs of handedness – the cockatiel *Nymphicus hollandicus*, which eats seeds on the ground rather than pick them up with its foot. Speculation is that, millions of years ago, when our distant ancestors had eyes on the sides of their heads like parrots, they had to perform a similar action which evolved eventually into handedness and our preference to be either right- or left-handed. Today, about 12 per cent of humans are left-handed, and 20 per cent are left-footed.

In a study at Canada's Simon Fraser University, Pacific tree frogs *Hyla regilla* were seen to show handedness. Escaping a predator, some jumped consistently 70° to the left. Whether this was the frog's 'choice' or was the result of the right hind limb being slightly longer than the left is unclear, but it could be another example of handedness linked to asymmetry in the body. Another is the crossbill *Loxia curvirostra*, which holds a pine cone with the foot that's on the same side as its lower mandible is bent.

When the light goes on and the cockroach heads for cover, there's a 56 per cent chance it'll turn to the right. In tests with a Y-shaped tube, researchers at Texas A&M University found that American cockroaches *Periplaneta americana* tended to go down the right-hand fork in over half the tests, no matter what smells were enticing them at the other end or whether they had intact antenna or not.

Female leatherback turtles *Dermochelys coriacea* tend to be right-flippered. When they have dug their nest and are about to deposit their eggs, the females place one rear flipper across the pit to shield it from view, and most use their right flipper.

Cottonmouth snakes *Agkistrodon piscivorus leucostoma* in south-eastern USA tend to coil in a clockwise fashion.

Mediterranean tortoises *Testudo hermanni* right themselves mainly on the right side.

THE WORLD'S OLDEST ANIMALS

Black corals *Leiopathes* that live in deep waters 300m (984ft) down are considered the oldest continuously living animals on Earth. Using radiocarbon dating methods, specimens from Hawaii were found to have been growing for at least 4,265 years. Gold corals *Gerardia* from the same site were dated at 2,742 years old and black corals of the genus *Antipatharia*, found in the Gulf of Mexico, are confirmed at over 2,000 years old. These corals grow exceedingly slowly, no more than a few micrometres per year.

Giant barrel sponges *Xestospongia muta,* living in the Caribbean, live for at least 2,300 years and the Antarctic sponge *Cinachyra antarctica* grows for more than 1,550 years.

The growth rings on a quahog clam *Arctica islandica,* found off the northern shore of Iceland, revealed that the mollusc was between 405 and 410 years old. It was a juvenile when James I replaced Elizabeth I as the English monarch, and when Shakespeare was writing *Hamlet, Othello, King Lear* and *Macbeth.*

A scarlet koi carp, a domesticated variety of the common carp *Cyprinus carpio,* was found to be 226 years old when she died. Hanako, as she was known, lived from 1751 to 1977, and her age was confirmed by examining the rings on her scales (like the rings on a tree). When she hatched, the establishment of the USA's Declaration of Independence was still twenty-five years away.

The Aldabara giant tortoise *Aldabrachelys gigantea,* known as Adwaita, died in 2006 in Kolkata (Calcutta) Zoo. Radio carbon dating of his shell revealed that he was 255 years old. The oldest living tortoise today is Esmeralda, a giant tortoise living on Bird Island in the Seychelles. She's about 170 years old.

Russian and Finnish researchers have confirmed that the slow-growing freshwater pearl mussel *Margaritifera margaritifera* lives for 210–250 years, and US scientists have discovered specimens of the red sea urchin *Strongylocentrotus franciscanus,* which is found on Pacific shores between Alaska and Baja California, that live for 200 years.

The world's oldest mammals could well be bowhead whales *Balaena mysticetus,* which live in Arctic and sub-Arctic waters. The discovery of ancient harpoon heads, some made of stone, buried in the flesh of whales caught more recently by Alaskan native whale hunters, together with evidence of changes of the level of aspartic acid in the whales' eye lens, has led researchers to suggest that these animals can live to over 200 years old. The oldest so far examined was 211 years old. Other whales have shorter lifespans. The oldest known age of a blue whale is 110 years, based on counting waxy laminates, like tree rings, in the ear-plug of whales. For a fin whale, the figure is 114 years.

The 3m (10ft) long, slow-growing, deep-sea tube-worm *Lamellibrachia luymesi* forms bush-like aggregations at cold hydrocarbon seeps 800m (2,625ft) down in the northern part of the Gulf of Mexico. The seeps, vents in the ocean floor where methane and hydrogen sulphide spew out, provide specialised bacteria with the raw materials to manufacture food. The tubeworm lives for at least 170 years – and possibly 250 years – relying on symbiotic bacteria in its tissues to supply it with nourishment.

By examining the rings and trace elements in the otoliths of the orange roughy or deep-sea perch *Hoplostethus atlanticus*, researchers have discovered this species of slow-growing, deep-sea fish lives to the grand old age of 125 to 156 years old. This brick-red fish is found in the Pacific, Atlantic and Indian oceans down to a depth of 1,800m (5,900ft).

Several species of shellfish seem to live to a ripe old age. Another clam, the large and edible saltwater geoduck *Panopea generosa*, native to the Pacific coast of North America, is not only the largest burrowing clam in the world (it grows up to 2m or 6.6ft long), but also one of the oldest. The oldest known specimen was 168 years old, but clams over 100 years old are rare.

A lobster *Homarus americanus* caught on the Newfoundland coast and known affectionately as George, was thought to be 140 years old. This would mean it was born in 1869, along with Neville Chamberlain, Mahatma Gandhi and Henri Matisse. It lived in an aquarium in a fish restaurant in New York for a couple of weeks, before being released back into the wild on the Maine coast in 2009.

Using the same techniques that pinned down the age of bowheads, Danish researchers have examined eyes from narwhals hunted by local folk in the waters off West Greenland, and discovered a female narwhal *Monodon monoceros* to have been 115 years old when she died.

The tuatara *Sphenodon* is a lizard-like, primitive reptile that lives only in the wild in New Zealand. It can be over 100 years old. A captive male at Southland Museum in Invercargill, known as Henry, mated for the first time at 111 years old. His mate was an octogenarian female who laid twelve eggs, of which eleven hatched successfully.

An old orca *Orcinus orca* matriarch, known as J-2 or Granny, is thought to be about 101 years old, as of 2012. She is one of the resident orcas of J pod, which patrols the waters around the San Juan Islands on the Pacific coast of North America. Like most experienced grannies, she is an adept babysitter and is one of the wild orcas to have appeared in the *Free Willy* movies.

The blind olm or cave salamander *Proteus anguinus* can live to over 100 years old, with an average age of sixty-nine years. This is three times more than would be expected for an animal of its size. Its pink snake-like body, with short legs, is no more than 30cm (12in.) long.

SHORT-LIVED

The Madagascan chameleon *Furcifer labordi* lives for just one year, of which it spends eight to nine months, i.e. three-quarters of its entire life, in its egg. When it hatches, it reaches sexual maturity within two months, reproduces and dies; a post-hatching lifespan of just four to five months. What's more, all the chameleons in this species synchronise their life cycle, so during the dry season the entire population is represented by developing eggs. These all hatch at the start of the wet season and at the end of the season the entire adult population dies.

Mayflies (Order: Ephemeroptera) spend the best part of a year as aquatic larvae, but in spring all the winged adults, triggered by a precise water temperature, emerge at exactly the same time. On the Tizsa River in Hungary, for example, they appear when the water temperature is exactly 21.5°C (70.7°F). They live for no more than an hour, or maybe a day, depending on the species, during which they have to mate and lay eggs before they die.

Free-living females of the parasitic nematode worm *Strongyloides ratti*, a gut parasite of the rat, live in the soil on average for three days and four and a half days at most, making them the world's shortest-lived nematode worms. This compares with a maximum of 403 days for its parasitic form – an eighty-fold difference – yet the two forms are genetically identical. The demise of the free-living form is due to an extraordinarily rapid aging process.

The pygmy coral reef goby *Eviota sigillata* from the Indo-Pacific region has the shortest lifespan of any known vertebrate. It lives for just fifty-nine days on average, but grows rapidly. Females produce three clutches during their short lifespan. The male stands guard and fans the eggs to ensure they receive sufficient oxygen. The hatching larvae float about in the ocean currents for three weeks, before settling on a coral reef where they mature in ten days and live for three and a half weeks, during which time they mate and the whole cycle starts again. This is a fish that lives fast and dies young.

Coming a close second is the turquoise killifish *Nothobranchius furzeri*, which must hatch out and breed before its seasonal rain pool in equatorial Africa disappears. It survives the dry season with desiccation-resistant eggs that can survive up to two years in the dried mud, but the adult fish dies after a maximum of twelve weeks.

FASHIONISTAS AND SOCIAL CLUBS

Alpha male or top-ranking savannah baboons *Papio cynocephalus* have high stress levels, on a par with low-ranked baboons. Life at the top may have its perks – access to food and females – but it comes at a cost, and pressures are different from those experienced lower down the pecking order. The alpha males have to continually preserve their status and engage in frequent mating, i.e. they try to keep everything, while the low-rankers are stressed because they have to fight for anything.

African lappet-faced vultures *Aegypius tracheliotus*, studied in Namibia by researchers from Nottingham University, were found to wear their status on their face. Increased blood flow to the bare skin on the head turns it bright red and, when many birds are feeding together and jostling for the best position at a carcass, those birds with the reddest skin are dominant. Those with pale skin are at the bottom of the pecking order. It's an instant way of updating a bird's status, much like we update our profiles on social networking sites.

The attractiveness of a zebra finch *Taeniopygia guttata* father influences the size and number of eggs produced by his daughter. The effect is based not on 'fitness', but appears to be related to the way the bird's mother perceives her mate – psychology rather than genetics. It means attractive dads have more grandchildren.

Male lark buntings *Calamospiza melanocorys* on the Colorado prairie must keep up with changing fashions. Females choose a mate who follows whatever is in vogue that year. The fashion is dictated by environmental or social pressure. If ground snakes *Sonora* are particularly numerous one year, for example, females might choose males that are likely to be the best protectors, a trait that's displayed by males having larger-than-normal coloured patches on the wings. The following year something entirely different could dictate the summer fashion.

What do you do if you're unattractive to the opposite sex? Male house finches *Carpodacus mexicanus*, a highly gregarious species that lives in southern Arizona, have a solution: they change clubs. Female house finches prefer males with red plumage, the result of carotenoid pigments in their diet, and they remain with their chosen one for a year and some-times for life, so any males with inferior yellow feathers don't really have a chance. However, if the unattractive males sense they're being out-classed, they look for another social group until they find a bunch of males that are less attractive, like them-selves. In this association they're more acceptable to females, and these previously spurned rovers do just as well as their suave counterparts in the matrimonial stakes. It goes to show that it's not who you are but where you are that counts in house finch society.

Killer whales *Orcinus orca* visit social clubs. In several places in the world – the Antarctica, Alaska, British Columbia and Iceland – there are huge gatherings of orcas, known as super-pods. The whales mill about, intermingling with members of other pods, catching up with old friends, flirting with the opposite sex and generally being sociable. Such a meeting place is Avacha Gulf on the Kamchatka Peninsula in the Russian Far East. Here, a hundred or so fish-eating orcas represent eight recognised pods, each with its own vocal dialect. It's thought the gatherings have little to do with protection or feeding; rather, they are times when potential mates can assess each other and whales generally can establish and maintain social bonds. They are also places where youngsters are born.

URBAN LIVING

Urban sparrows *Passer domesticus*, great tits *Parus major* and blackbirds *Turdus merula* sing at a higher frequency than their country cousins, probably to cut through the low-frequency sounds of the city – but this may be only part of the reason. Birds singing in quiet places without the noise of traffic or machinery also raise the pitch of their song. Birds in woodlands must cope with reflections off trees and leaves when judging distances, and locating one another when there is no line of sight. Birds in cities must do the same, except the urban jungle consists of buildings, alleys and open spaces. It seems that shifting the pitch of their song is one way to get their message through. For birds, like male great tits, this is a problem, for when female great tits are most fertile they are more attracted to low-pitched songs. They will even cheat on a mate if his song is too high. It means if urban male great tits want to be sure of obtaining and keeping a mate, their territories must be in the quieter parts of town, away from main roads.

Compared to their country cousins, urban black bears *Ursus americanus* are 30 per cent overweight due to picking through rubbish bins. They become pregnant at a younger age – two to three years old compared to the more usual seven to eight years old – and generally meet an early and violent end, due mainly to collisions with vehicles. They do not necessarily learn these bad habits from their mother, but sometimes from unrelated 'bad influence' bears, or they just pick them up themselves. When they do, they become life-long problem bears.

When living in the country, the odorous house ant *Tapinoma sessile* lives in hollow acorns in small colonies of fifty to a hundred workers with a single queen – and it bothers nobody. However, when it heads into town, it forms super-colonies of up to five million individuals and thousands of queens, and they go on the rampage, stealing food from other ants and invading buildings, from which they're extremely difficult to remove. Why the ants change their behaviour in the urban setting is a mystery, but you know when they're there: the ant gets its common name from smelling of coconuts when crushed.

Many animals, especially waterborne insects, are confused by the many dark, shiny surfaces in towns and cities. To them a black plastic bag, tarmac road surface, oil spill or a dark flat roof looks like a pond. The key is polarised light, which reflects off bodies of water, amongst other things. A dragonfly (Infraorder: Anisoptera), whose early life stages depend on water, orients toward strong sources of polarised light, but can find itself confronted with something altogether different. Stoneflies (Order: Plecoptera) have been seen to lay their eggs on tarmac, and a female water beetle (Family: Belostomatidae) was once observed to deposit her eggs on the roof of a red car.

Bats (Order: Chiroptera) also 'see' all smooth surfaces as water. In experiments at the Max Planck Institute for Ornithology, many different species of bats were presented with flat, smooth surfaces of metal, wood and plastic, and time and time again they would swoop down and try to drink. Even though their eyes and senses of touch and smell must have told them it wasn't water, their brain appears to be hard-wired to spot anything resembling water. Bats use their echolocation systems to locate water, for they need to drink and they often catch insects over water. However, it means that skylights, car roofs and other smooth surfaces could be very confusing for a bat.

Across Britain, 60,000 metric tonnes of birdseed is dished out annually to garden birds, especially during the winter months, and in the USA $3 billion is spent annually on bird food. Most birds benefit from this free handout. More survive the winter, they breed earlier and have more offspring, but there is a downside. Blue tits *Cyanistes caeruleus* and great tits *Parus major* fed peanut cake through the winter have significantly smaller brood sizes in spring, and a study in the USA showed that Florida scrub jays *Aphelocoma coerulescens* fed with birdseed during the winter bred too early, so the natural foods needed by their chicks were unavailable and they didn't survive. If resident birds fatten up in winter, breed earlier and get a head start on exploiting the naturally available foods, they are going to be stiff competition for migrants returning from the tropics. It has led some ornithologists to discourage winter feeding.

Crows *Corvus* recognise human faces. A bus driver in Washington State nearly lost her job because she regularly fed her neighbourhood crows and the birds started to follow her to work. Similarly, researchers at the University of Washington in Seattle found that when they trapped crows to ring them, it was nigh on impossible to trap them a second time. They seemed to recognise the trappers so the researchers decided to test whether the crows really did recognise people, undertaking a series of theatrical experiments to do so. The researchers wore rubber masks: one was a grotesque face, dubbed 'the caveman', and another was a likeness of Dick Cheney, former vice-president of the USA. People wearing the Dick Cheney mask were neutral and did not interact with the birds. People wearing the caveman mask deployed a cannon-net system and captured a handful of birds for ringing. For the next three years, people wearing the masks visited the same sites. Those wearing the Dick Cheney mask were ignored, but anybody wearing the caveman mask was dive-bombed and mobbed, even when the individual researchers were of different heights, had distinctive walking gaits and were walking amongst crowds of people. The birds focused only on the caveman face, associating this face with somebody that might do them harm; and they remembered it for a long time. Similarly, northern mockingbirds *Mimus polyglottos* at a University of Florida campus were shown to recognise individuals who threaten their nests, and in Paris feral pigeons recognised an individual that chased them and ignored the person that let them be; even though the two people swapped lab coats, the birds had recognised their faces.

Size for size, songbirds that move into our towns and cities tend to have significantly bigger brains than those that live exclusively in the country. Research carried out at the Evolutionary Biology Centre in Sweden suggests that birds that flourish in urban areas have a greater ability to adapt to unnatural environments and solve problems, such as a serious lack of trees, the lure of plate-glass windows and whether to eat novel foods that have been discarded in roads and on pavements.

European blackbirds *Turdus merula* living in cities migrate shorter distances than country birds. Urban blackbirds in northern Europe, which started to come into towns in the 1930s, remain very close to their summer nest sites in winter, while forest dwellers head off to sunnier climes, some reaching North Africa. The research team from Sheffield University believe the warmer towns and availability of food has seduced blackbirds to become more sedentary, and it could be a first step to the formation of two separate species – an urban and a rural blackbird.

Birds in cities are more macho than their country cousins, and it's all to do with light. Streetlights play havoc with natural rhythms but this can have advantages. Researchers at the Max Planck Institute for Ornithology have found that male blue tits *Cyanistes caeruleus*, together with three other songbird species living near streetlights at the edge of a Viennese forest start to sing up to ten minutes earlier than those living in the forest's interior. Females find this attractive. The early singers are probably deemed fitter and they have twice the number of extramarital liaisons than those in the country. It also helps one-year-old males: normally, these youngsters rarely get a look-in with the loose females, but those living near streetlights had as much success as the older males.

In Brighton, on the south coast of England, the droppings from gulls are blocking the photosensors on the town's 19,000 streetlights, so they remain on throughout the day as well as the night. Some lights have been on for several months.

HOME SWEET HOME

The veined octopus *Amphioctopus marginatus*, which lives in the coastal waters of northern Sulawesi and Bali, has been found by researchers from Australia's Museum Victoria to adopt a bizarre home. The octopus picks up half coconut shells that have been discarded by people and then tiptoes away on stiffened arms, stilt-walking like a spider, with the shells slung below its body. It might carry them more than 20m (65ft) away to a place where it feels relatively safe. If it has one shell it turns it over and hides underneath it, and if it has two halves it assembles them like the original coconut and hides inside, the suckers on its arms holding the two halves in place. The habit probably started when the octopus, which lives on a muddy seabed with nowhere to hide, used bivalve shells for protection. It switched to coconuts when they became abundant. It's the first example of a cephalopod using a tool.

Red groupers *Epinephalus morio* in the Gulf of Mexico and along the south-east coast of the USA excavate complex three-dimensional holes in the sand. They carry sand from the centre of their pit and expel it from their mouths and gills on the periphery, and using their tails they brush away the sand on the floor to expose the bare rock below. The bare rock encourages the growth of corals and sponges, and the holes provide hideaways for all sorts of sea creatures, such as cleaner shrimps, which divest the groupers of parasites and dead skin. The holes also attract a potential meal – fish – so the groupers become real couch potatoes. They have no need to chase after prey as it all comes to them.

The Darwin bark spider *Caerostris darwini* of Madagascar builds some of the world's largest known orb webs. Anchor lines can stretch for 25m (82ft) and the web itself can cover an area of 2.8 sq. metres (30 sq. ft). It is usually built over a river or lake, and one web was found to contain thirty-two mayflies that had been trapped in a single day. Females of the species responsible for these mega-webs are no more than 2cm (0.79in.) across and males are much smaller, but their silk is the strongest known of any spider, ten times tougher than a similar piece of Kevlar, a synthetic fibre used in body armour. The spider was discovered in 2009, along with a klep-toparasitic fly that steals some of the prey caught in the web.

The dark, warm and humid atmosphere inside a termite mound ought to be a haven for harmful bacteria and fungi, but it's not. Termites produce an antimicrobial enzyme in their saliva that they spread over their bodies and the walls of their home. The enzyme attacks the cell walls of microbes, making them leaky and susceptible to attacks from the termites' other antimicrobial agents.

Every night in sugar cane plantations near the town of São Simão in south-central Brazil, the ant *Forelius pusillus* demonstrates some remarkably selfless behaviour. As darkness falls, the colony seals the entrances to its underground nest with sand, but not all the ants are safely inside. To be certain that the entrance is sealed tight from the likes of maraud-ing army ants and other predators, a handful of ants remain outside to shore up the defences. It's a suicide mission, for most will not survive the night outside the nest. These ants will have sacrificed their own lives for the good of the colony. While many social animals, such as bees, will sacrifice themselves when confronted with an immediate threat, this is the first recognised case of an animal sacrificing itself in a premeditated and pre-emptive way.

There comes a time when a honeybee *Apis mellifera* colony becomes too overcrowded, so two-thirds of the workers and the old queen leave their home and look for pastures new. At first the swarm hangs on a nearby tree while hundreds of scout bees search for a new nest site. They come back with news of about ten to twenty sites and then dance: this is the bees' way of conveying information about food sources and new home sites. The length of each dance relates to the quality of the site, and the scouts don't exaggerate their claims. They have an inbuilt ability to judge a site and they give an honest performance: if the site is mediocre, the dance is short; if it is high-quality real estate, the dance is long. The other members of the colony read the dance and they vote with their feet. Increasingly more scouts visit the better sites and when it reaches a critical threshold they all move to the chosen new home, the entire process being strictly democratic. However, if two sites have equal value, a little coercing and election-rigging takes place. Bees from one site inhibit the dances of bees from the other site by head-butting them, and the more the scouts are head-butted the less likely the colony is to choose their site.

In autumn, the larvae of leaf miner moths that burrow into the leaf tissues of broadleaved trees are likely to find themselves out of a home and short on food as the leaves turn yellow or red and then die. *Phyllonorycter blancardella,* however, has a way to prolong its leaf's life, at least the part of the leaf closest to it. Bacteria in the larvae cause that part of the leaf to emain green and fully photosynthetic, so the leaf miner is surrounded by an island of green, while the rest of the leaf wilts. By having this relationship with the bacterium, the leaf miner effectively buys itself an extra month to grow, pupate and maybe even sneak in another generation before winter.

Australia's great desert skink *Liopholis kintorei* is an unexpected but enthusiastic homemaker. It excavates elaborate burrows, the network some-times 13m (43ft) across and featuring multiple entrances and dedicated latrine areas, and it might be occupied continuously for up to seven years. The surprise is that it does not dig alone. Close family members maintain the tunnels, with parents and children working alongside each other. This is the first time a lizard has been recorded constructing a family house.

ALMOST HUMAN (1)

Chimpanzees *Pan troglodytes* associate high-pitched sounds with light colours and low-pitched sounds with dark colours, just like humans do.

Young female chimpanzees play with 'dolls'. Chimps pick up sticks for all kinds of uses, from warfare to obtaining food, but young females in Uganda's Kibale National Park have been seen to cradle sticks in their arms or tucked between their abdomen and thigh. The behaviour, according to Harvard University researchers, looks uncommonly like a human child with a doll.

Common chimpanzees beat their wives. Male chimps frequently and brutally hit females in their troop, sometimes with branches. It is thought to be a way, according to research at Boston University, that dominant males ensure females do not mate with other males; a form of sexual coercion. Females who received the most beatings turned out to be the most fertile and twice as likely to become pregnant as females who escaped the violence. However, analysis of hormone levels in persecuted females revealed that they were highly stressed, a situation that could lead to stomach ulcers and a suppressed disease-fighting (immune) system.

If a male chimpanzee shares his meat with another male, he has probably recruited an ally who will come to his aid should any fighting break out. He might also share with a receptive female in exchange for sexual favours, but a surprise came when researchers from the Max Planck Institute for Evolutionary Biology observed males sharing meat with non-receptive females. Chimps, it seems, might plan ahead.

Near the West African village of Bossou, in the Republic of Guinea, where prey is scarce, male chimpanzees raid papaya plantations and offer the fruit to females – crops for sex! The same groups of chimps use stones to crack open nuts.

A trait they share with us is that chimpanzees kill for land. Gangs of male chimpanzees in Uganda's Kibale National Park go on patrol every couple of weeks and make surprise incursions into a neighbouring territory. They're members of the Ngogo troop, a large group of chimpanzees which occupies a high-quality habitat, but which is intent on taking more. If they hear the calls of a neighbour, they advance rapidly and silently. Often as not it's a solitary male, which they kill by beating and biting it – and sometimes eat it. Eventually, the neighbours are either eliminated or move away, and Ngogo chimps take over the territory and expand their own foraging range. It seems that chimpanzees are not aggressive when they're weak, but they are when they're strong, which makes the Ngogo troop the neighbours from hell.

Chimpanzees are not all bad: they can show self-less behaviour, too. In the Taï National Park in the Côte D'Ivoire, a young chimpanzee lost his mother to anthrax, but a young male in the troop adopted the orphan. The older male shared his night nest, carried the youngster on his back, waited for him to catch up and shared his meal of *Coula* nuts, which had been carefully cracked open with rocks – all behaviours usually seen in mother chimpanzees. During the past three decades, researchers from the

Max Planck Institute for Evolutionary Anthropology have observed eighteen cases of adoption, which varied between three months and five years, and ten of them were by males, even though normally male chimps have little to do with their own offspring. Whether this apparently selfless behaviour on the part of the adoptive males are cases of altruism, or whether it is a male chimp investing in a future alliance or grooming partner, or simply mistaking the offspring for his own, is not clear.

Chimpanzees and African elephants *Loxodonta africana* appear to grieve over dead relatives. On one occasion in 2003, an elderly elephant in Kenya collapsed and was then helped to her feet several times by others in the herd. The following day she died, but the herd would not leave her. They kept a vigil for over a week. Similarly in 2008, a female chimpanzee became ill at a Scottish safari park. Three other adults, including her daughter, gathered around her, grooming her and sleeping next to her instead of their usual sleeping areas. Eventually she died, but her daughter would not leave her during the entire night. The keepers removed the body the following morning and the chimpanzees were noticeably subdued for over a week. At a wildlife orphanage in Zambia, a chimpanzee mother was seen to carry the dead body of her sixteen-month-old infant for more than a day. Then, she placed it on the ground and touched its face and neck repeatedly, before carrying it to a group of chimpanzees that looked carefully at the body. The next day, the mother no longer carried the dead infant.

Capuchin monkeys *Cebus* go on strike. In tests in the laboratory, individuals who have seen other monkeys receiving a greater reward for solving the same task, down tools and walk out, refusing to take any further part in the trial.

UNEXPECTED PREDATORS

Bonobos *Pan paniscus* have long had a gentle, laid-back image, making love not war, but observations of these apes in the Congo basin by researchers from the Max Planck Institute for Evolutionary Biology show a much darker side. Until now, their common chimpanzee *P. troglodytes* cousins were considered the bloodthirsty species. Gangs of male chimps hunt and eat monkeys, but now bonobos have being seen out hunting too, not in groups of males, but in gangs of females. While male common chimps dominate females, hunt for meat and murder males from other troops, the reverse is true for bonobos. It's the females who take charge. The researchers report six hunting expeditions by female bonobos, some hunts involving a male or a juvenile as well. Red-tailed monkeys *Cercopithecus ascanius* were their victims.

ALMOST HUMAN (2)

Male Indian Ocean bottlenose dolphins *Tursiops aduncus* at Shark Bay on the coast of Western Australia join gangs, according to University of Massachusetts scientists, and live in a complex open society without territorial boundaries in which they must be smart to survive. The alliances can be at several levels. The basic gang is two or three dolphins. They appropriate an individual female who is ready to mate, and guard her closely for up to a month. The second level of alliances can see between four and fourteen males forming gangs that raid other medium-sized groups intent on stealing their females or defend against attacks from other gangs. These relationships can last for months and even years; one seven-strong gang still meet together after seventeen years. At the third level they call in the troops and even bigger groups are formed;

these 'armies' defend their females against other large groups. The battles can see twenty or more males biting and bashing with snouts and tails over the right to mate with a single female. However, in order to live in this way, the dolphins must be intelligent enough to be able to work out whether other dolphins they encounter are allies or a threat. Unlike other smart animals, such as chimpanzees, which have well-defined and defended groups and an 'us against them' form of aggression, dolphins must decide whether to be friendly and form an alliance or to be aggressive and fight; apparently, they even switch sides. It's been likened to a TV soap opera, where one has to keep tabs on who is doing what with whom in order to decide whether to remain friends or become foes. The number of relationships a male has to monitor is mind-boggling, and there is always the uncertainty that a dolphin has switched sides since he was last encountered. The social skills needed to live in this kind of society are likely to have contributed to dolphins' large brains, and this multilevel system of social groups is shared with only one other animal on Earth – us.

Female dolphins also benefit from having friends. The females of Shark Bay have more calves that survive to three years old, the age at which young dolphins become independent of their mothers, if they hang out with females who have successfully raised their young to that age.

Dolphins meet and greet in the open sea. Researchers from the University of St Andrews have been following groups of dolphins along the north-east coast of Scotland – the most northerly pods of common bottlenose dolphins *Tursiops truncatus*. When travelling, a dolphin pod is usually relatively quiet, but when they meet other dolphins a 'spokesperson' from each group, possibly an older and wiser individual, emits signature whistle-like sounds. The conversation essentially names the individuals and probably exchanges basic information, such as sex, age, state of health, and friend or foe. After this formal greeting ceremony other members of the group join in and they all swim along together, the excited conversations gradually trailing off before the dolphins become quiet again.

Bottlenose dolphins are not always the cute and playful sea mammals with the winning smile that we've come to love. Aside from being efficient and resourceful predators, they are also murderers. Off the Scottish coast and in the western Pacific, dolphins have been seen to attack and kill harbour porpoises *Phocoena phocoena* for no apparent reason. The porpoises are chased, rammed repeatedly and drowned by gangs of mainly juvenile male dolphins. In one particularly vicious attack, witnessed by researchers from Okeanis, Moss Landing, three dolphins corralled a lone porpoise, to be joined by seven others who rammed their victim to death. Two dolphins remained behind and played with the carcass, before pushing it towards the researchers' boat, as if to say, 'We're finished with it, it's your turn'. Competition for food has been ruled out as a cause, as the two species tend to go for different prey, but the fact they are mostly young males is thought to be significant. Young males have trouble getting access to females during the breeding season, as gangs of older males chase them off. It could be that they are taking out their frustrations on anything that swims by and, in these cases, their unwitting victims are porpoises.

DOLPHINS TO THE RESCUE

In 1983, a pod of pilot whales *Globicephala* ran aground on the ebb tide at Tokerau Beach on New Zealand's North Island. Local people came out to try to keep the animals alive until the tide came in, but the whales were having trouble knowing which way was the open sea. Up popped a pod of dolphins (Family: Delphinidae). They swam into the shallows and herded the pilot whales away from the shore, saving seventy-six of the pod of eighty. There were many witnesses, but this was not a lone incident. A similar event had occurred at Whangarei Harbour just five years previously.

In 1996, a British tourist was on board a boat off the Egyptian coast in the Gulf of Aqaba. The boat had stopped so the passengers could watch a pod of dolphins. Several tourists went into the water with them and one stayed longer than the rest. Suddenly, a shark attacked him – and other sharks were moving in. Three of the dolphins immediately swam around the man, slapping the sea's surface with their tails and flippers, until he could be pulled from the water.

In October 2004, a group of four swimmers were in the water near Whangarei on New Zealand's North

Island. A pod of dolphins arrived and the people, who included a lifeguard and his daughter and friends, thought they were being playful, but the dolphins began to swim in gradually tighter circles, 'herding' the swimmers together. Then the man spotted a 3m (10ft) long great white shark *Carcharodon carcharias* no more than 2m (6.6ft) away. The dolphins continued to circle them for about forty minutes, until the shark lost interest and left. The dolphins also disappeared and the group of swimmers was able to swim the 100m (about 100 yards) back to the beach. Another lifeguard witnessed the entire event.

In August 2007, a surfer was attacked at Marina State Park off Monterey, California. The shark – probably a 3.7–4.6m (12–15ft) great white shark – bit him and his board three times, peeling the skin off his back and biting into his leg right to the bone. Dolphins that had been swimming in the surf suddenly turned up and swam around the surfer, keeping the shark at bay. He was able to remount his board and surf back to the beach, where prompt first aid saved his life.

In June 2008, the *Nicole Louis* fishing boat was sailing off Burias Island in the Visayan Sea when it was hit by Typhoon Frank. The boat sank and most of the crew clung to a raft or anything they found that could float. They then saw a dolphin drag and push one of their crewmates, who had failed to find a float, towards the island. Unfortunately, the storm caused both the man and the dolphin to drown, and their bodies were found later on an island beach. The fishermen are convinced the dolphin died trying to save their friend.

The actor Dick Van Dyke claimed on a US television show that he too had been saved by dolphins or porpoises. He was on his 3m (10ft) long surfboard at Virginia Beach on the east coast of the USA, when he dozed off and drifted out to sea, out of sight of land. He started to paddle with the swell but was suddenly surrounded by fins. He thought they were sharks and that he would die, but they were dolphins and they pushed him all the way to shore.

A curious event occurred off the Somali coast in April 2009. Pirates were pursuing several Chinese merchant ships as they passed the Gulf of Aden, when a large pod of hundreds of dolphins suddenly surfaced between the pirates and the merchants.

The pirates turned back and the Chinese ships continued on their way home. Although the arrival of the dolphins was probably coincidence, when it comes to dolphins one can't help but wonder.

In February 2011, a pet Doberman dog went missing from a house on Marco Island, Florida. Unknown to the owner, it had fallen into a local canal and couldn't get out. Another resident heard a great commotion coming from the canal and, when she took a look, she saw a dolphin making a lot of noise and splashing. It seemed to be trying to raise the alarm. The rescuer was able to reach the dog, which had found a corner of sand in shallow water at low tide, and take it to safety.

LIONS TO THE RESCUE

About 560km (350 miles) south-west of Addis Ababa, in Ethiopia, a twelve-year-old girl was abducted and beaten by a gang of men who were trying to force her to marry one of them. She had been missing for about a week when the local police found her on the outskirts of Binet Genet – but what was waiting with her was the biggest surprise. A pride of lions had chased off the gang and had been guarding her for the best part of the day. It's been suggested that her crying may have sounded like a whimpering cub, and so the lions did not attack her. The pride itself was of Abyssinian lions, a rare subspecies *Panthera leo abyssinica* whose males have dark, sometimes black, manes. When the police arrived the lions sloped off, leaving the girl safe. Not far away, about three months later, lions showed their true colours when they attacked and killed twenty people and numerous livestock, causing people to flee from their homes. So why they didn't attack the young girl is a mystery. As the police officer who found her said, 'It's a miracle.'

HUMPBACK TO THE RESCUE

At the beginning of 2009, orca researchers Robert Pitman and John Durban were watching a pod of orcas *Orcinus orca* 'wave-washing'. They were swimming together at an ice floe on which a Weddell seal *Leptonychotes weddellii* was resting and they succeeded in washing it into the water. Just then, a group of humpback whales *Megaptera novaeangliae* appeared. The seal swam to one that was swimming on its side and leapt onto its ribbed throat, nestling into the whale's armpit. When a wave threatened to wash the seal back into the sea, the humpback moved its huge flipper and pushed the seal back in place. A few minutes later the seal took off and swam rapidly to another, safer ice floe. The researchers speculate that the seal might have triggered the whale's maternal instinct, as if she had a calf to protect.

In California's Monterey Bay in May 2012, a BBC film crew was filming a grey whale *Eschrichtius robustus* and calf, when killer whales attacked the two whales. Suddenly, a pod of humpback whales appeared and began to trumpet, dive and slap their pectoral fins and powerful tails at the killers, but their attempts to see off the attacking pod were to no avail. The mother was separated from her calf and the calf killed. Nevertheless, the humpbacks continued to harass any killer whales that approached. The entire event played out over seven hours.

WHAT ON EARTH?

In natural history and related sciences, words – especially the names of animals, whether formal or informal – can sometimes appear a little strange, so in this section of the book we delve into the naturalist's dictionary and pick out some of the more wacky examples. As often as not, the name reflects how we view that animal. Scientific names reflect some aspect of the animal's actual make-up or behaviour, while common names sometimes give the animal human characteristics, but whenever and wherever names are assigned they are sure to bring a smile.

The 'blue doctor' *Rhetus periander* is an exquisite tropical butterfly from Central and South America. The upper surfaces of the male's wings are iridescent blue with black wing margins and conspicuous spots of reddish-orange on the tail-like trailing edge of the hind wings.

The 'blue heart playboy' *Philodeudorix caerulea* is a butterfly from West Africa's dry forests and savannah.

The 'bishop's mitre' *Aelia acuminata* is a European shield bug with a pointed head.

The 'by-the-wind sailor' *Velella velella* is a hydrozoan with a membranous 'sail' that is blown across the surface of the world's oceans.

The 'alewife' *Alosa pseudoharengus* is a species of herring; and those in landlocked waters are called 'sawbellies'.

'Chuck-will's-widow' *Caprimulgus carolinensis* is a nocturnal bird in the nightjar family that lives in south-eastern USA.

The 'chimney-sweeper' *Odezia atrata* is a sooty-black, day-flying moth from Europe.

The 'cobbler wobbegong' *Sutorectus tentaculatus* is a rarely seen shark from Western Australia and South Australia, which is camouflaged so well that it blends in with its background of coral, rocks and seaweed.

'Cookie-cutters' are small sharks *Isistius* that take distinctive circular bites out of larger marine animals, such as whales, dolphins and tuna.

'Cousin German' *Protolampra sobrina* is a rare European moth whose caterpillars feed first on bilberry and ling, and then birch leaves.

The 'flip flop' *Leptosia alcesta* is a delicate wood white butterfly found in Africa.

The 'foolish swift' *Borbo fatuellus* is a brown butter-fly from tropical Africa.

'Forkbeard' can be any number of creatures, including two species of fish: a species of Atlantic hake, known as the great forkbeard *Phycis blennoides* and the lesser forkbeard or tadpole fish *Raniceps raninus*.

The 'gag' is not a joke but a species of grouper *Mycteroperca microlepis*.

The 'hellbender' is a giant salamander *Cryptobranchus alleganiensis* that lives in rivers in eastern USA.

The 'jolthead porgy' is an ocean-going sea bream, and known in Bermuda as the 'blue bone pory' *Calamus bajonado*.

The 'morose sailor' *Neptis morosa* is a brown West African butterfly with white splashes on the upper surface of its wings.

The 'noseburn wanderer' *Mestra amymone* is a butterfly found from Costa Rica to South Dakota. It has grey to light brown upper surfaces to its wings, with an orange strip along the trailing edge, and pale orange underneath.

The 'one pip policeman' *Coeliades anchises* is a butterfly that is to be found along the east coast of Africa, from South Africa to Ethiopia. It gets its common name from the single smudge of white on the underside of each wing.

A 'rainbow runner' *Elagatis bipinnulata* is a marine fish in the jack family. It's sometimes seen rubbing itself on the rough skin of sharks, probably to remove external parasites.

'Sliders' are freshwater terrapins *Trachemys scripta*. The red-eared subspecies, also known as the red-eared terrapin, has become a successful alien species wherever people have kept them as pets and then released them into the wild.

The 'snowflake' *Leucidia brephos* is a wispy-white butterfly to be seen flying in clearings where fallen trees have allowed light to penetrate to the forest floor. It lives in the Amazon rainforest and other forests in South and Central America.

'Stargazers' (Family: Uranoscopidae) are shallow-water fish with eyes on the top of their heads and an upward-pointing mouth in a large head. They leap up to catch prey.

The 'sungazer' *Cordylus giganteus* is a spiny girdle lizard from South Africa. It gets its common name from the way it sits in its burrow entrance and faces the sun.

'Sweet William' is a colloquial name for both the gummy shark *Mustelus antarcticus*, from southern Australia's temperate waters, and the tope or soup-fin shark *Galeorhinus galeus*, found worldwide in temperate and sub-tropical waters, about which Welsh naturalist Thomas Pennant wrote in his *British Zoology* in 1776, 'Its skin and flesh has an offensive rank smell; therefore we suppose Mr Dale [physician and geologist] gave it ironically the title of Sweet William.'

'Unctuous sucker' is a moniker given to a small tadpole-shaped fish *Liparis liparis*. It received its name in the nineteenth century, reflecting its sliminess.

'Watering pots' (Family: Penicillidae) are bivalve marine molluscs, whose shells look like a very tall magician's hat; where the magician's head would fit is a perforated disc that looks just like the head of a watering can.

NOT WHAT'S ON THE TIN

The ant bear is not an ant or a bear but the name given to two animals that eat ants and termites – Africa's aardvark *Orycteropus afer* and South America's giant anteater *Myrmecophaga tridactyla*.

The skunk bear is not a skunk or a bear, but one of the common names of the wolverine or glutton *Gulo gulo*, the largest land-living member of the weasel family. It has a reputation for ferocity and is very capable of killing animals bigger than itself, including adult deer, although it relies more on carrion, especially in winter and early spring. It lives mainly in the great boreal forests of North America and Eurasia.

The woolly bear is not a bear but the caterpillar of moths in the family Arctiidae.

The ant lion is not an ant or a lion but the larval form of a lacewing-like insect *Myrmeleon* spp. In sandy areas, the larva digs a circular pit and then conceals itself in the bottom with just its formidable jaws protruding from the sand. It then waits. The slope of the pit and the loose sand are carefully designed to collapse should an ant fall in, so it is difficult to climb out. The larva also throws sand at the trapped animal so it has little chance of escape.

The bee wolf is not a bee or a wolf, but a predatory wasp *Philanthus* that specialises in catching bees.

The cow ant is not a cow or an ant but a wasp. The wingless females are furry and resemble ants, and are more generally known as velvet ants in the family Mutillidae.

THE FROG WITH SELF-CLEANING FEET

The seahorse *Hippocampus* is not an equid, but it does live in the sea. It's a bony fish with a head shaped like that of a horse. It lives mainly in shallow waters amongst seaweeds and in sea grass meadows, coral reefs and mangroves.

The wolf eel *Anarrhichthys ocellatus* is not a wolf or an eel but a stocky, eel-shaped fish with powerful jaws. It scrunches up sea urchins, shellfish and the occasional fish, and can give a painful bite if disturbed. It lives on rocky reefs in the northern part of the Pacific Ocean.

The armyworm is not a worm but the caterpillar stage of the moth *Spodoptera*. Plagues of this caterpillar can wipe out an entire crop in a single night, bringing starvation to already hungry lands. Similarly, inchworms (Family: Geometridae) and cutworms (Family: Noctuidae) are not worms but the caterpillars of moths.

Cuttlefish (Order: Spiidae), silverfish *Lepisma saccharina*, starfish (Class: Asteroidea), crayfish (Family: Astacidae) and jellyfish (Phylum: Cnidaria) are not fish but a cephalopod mollusc, insect, echinoderm, crustacean and coelenterate respectively; and sea cucumbers (Class: Holothuroidea), sea lilies (Class: Criniodea) and sea anemones (Order: Actiniaria) are not plants but an echinoderm, a crinoid (echinoderm) and a coelenterate.

THE WOODLOUSE

The humble woodlouse (Suborder: Oniscidea) is not actually a single species but more than 3,000 species, of which only a handful are commonly seen. Of these, only a few roll into a ball when disturbed, but this behaviour, together with a superficial resemblance to pigs, has given rise to an extraordinary number of nicknames. In the English county of Devon alone, an enthusiast collected thirty-four different names, and there are more than 150 used throughout Britain. Even more crop up elsewhere in the world. Here are just a few:

Armadillo bugs	Carpenters
Bibble-bugs	Cafners
Billy-buttons	Cheese logs
Bloodsuckers	Cheesy bugs
Boat-builders	Chizzlers
Buckle-bugs	Chucky pigs
Butcher boys	Chuggy pigs
Butchy boys	Coffin cutters

Cudworms

Curdworms

Doodlebugs

Eerie bugs

Footballers

Gramersows

Gramfy groogers

Grandfathers

Granny greys

Granny pickers

Grey sows

Leatherjackets

Loafers

Monkey peas

Parson's pigs

Pea balls

Pill bugs

Pissebedden

Pollydishwashers

Potato bugs

Roll up bugs

Roly-polys

Slaters

Slater beetles

Slater bugs

Scabby sow bugs

Shoelaces

Sink-lices

Sow bugs

Tanks

Tiggy hogs

Wood bugs

ANIMAL COLLECTIVE NOUNS

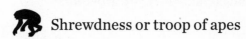 Shrewdness or troop of apes

Tribe, congress or a flange (from BBC1's *Not the Nine o'Clock News*) of baboons

Cete or colony of badgers

Battery of barracudas

Cloud of bats

 Sleuth or sloth of bears

Lodge of beavers

Flight, grist, hive or swarm of bees

Congregation, dissimulation, flight, flock, plump, knob, volary or volery of game birds

Sedge or siege of bitterns, cranes or herons

 Sounder or singular of boar

Chain of bobolinks

Brace or clash of buck

Obstinacy of buffalo

Bellowing of bullfinches

Rabble, flutter or swarm of butterflies

Wake of buzzards

 Caravan or train of camels

Army of caterpillars

Clowder, clutter, glare, glorying, pounce,
dout or nuisance of cats

Kendle, kindle, intrigue or litter of kittens

 Cartload of chimpanzees

Coalition of cheetahs

Clatter of choughs

Bed of clams or oysters

Quiver of cobras

Intrusion of cockroaches

Lap of cod

Bury of conies

Cover or raft of coots

Gulp of cormorants

Band, train or pack of coyotes

Cast or consortium of crabs

 Bask, float or congregation of
crocodiles or alligators

Murder, horde, parcel or storytelling of crows

Herd, leash, rangale or parcel of deer

Bevy of roe deer

 Pod of dolphins, porpoises or whales

Trip of dotterel

Bevy, cote, dole, dule or flight of doves

Brace, flock, flush, paddling, raft or team of ducks

Badelynge (pronounced 'bad-ling'), brace, safe,
sord, sore or waddling of ducks on the ground

Paddling, bunch or raft of ducks on water

Fling of dunlins

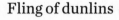 Aerie or convocation of eagles

Swarm, bed or fry of eels

Herd, memory or parade of elephants

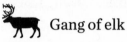 Gang of elk

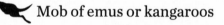 Mob of emus or kangaroos

Cast of falcons

Business, cast or fesnying of ferrets

Charm of finches or hummingbirds

School, shoal, draught and nest of fish

Catch, drought or haul of caught fish

Stand or flamboyance of flamingos

Business, swarm or cloud of flies

Lead, leash or skulk of foxes

Army, knot or colony of frogs

 Gaggle, flock, skein (when flying) or
wedge (in V-formation) of geese

Corps or tower of giraffes

Cloud, horde or swarm of gnats

Implausibility of gnus

Charm, troubling or glint of goldfish

Band of gorillas

Covey or pack of grouse

Bizarre of guillemots

Screech of gulls

Confusion of guinea fowl

Drove, down, husk, leash, trace,
trip or warren of hares

Cast, boil (when spiralling) or
kettle (when flying) of hawks

Array or prickle of hedgehogs

Army or shoal of herring

Crash or bloat of hippos

Bike of hornets

Clan or cackle of hyenas

Party, band or scold of jays

Smack, brood or swarm of jellyfish

Deceit of lapwings

Ascension or exultation of larks

Leap of leopards

Flock of lice

Pride, sault or sowse of lions

Lounge of lizards

Plague or swarm of locusts

Tiding, gulp, murder or charm of magpies

Sord of mallards in flight

Richness of martens

Mischief or horde of mice or rats

Shoal, school, swarm or steam of minnows

Company, labour or movement of moles

Cartload, troop, barrel or tribe of monkeys

Scourge of mosquitoes

Watch of nightingales

Bevy, raft, family or romp of otters

Parliament or stare of owls

Company or pandemonium of parrots

Covey or bew of partridges

Muster, pride or ostentation of peacocks

Pod of pelicans

Rookery or parcel of penguins

Nest or nye of pheasants

Nide of pheasant chicks

Bouquet of pheasants taking off

Flight, flock or kit of pigeons

Congregation of plovers

Wing of plovers in flight

Chine of polecats

Prickle of porcupines

Passel of possums

Coterie of prairie dogs

Covey of ptarmigans

 Bury, down, drove, husk, leash,
trace or trip of rabbits

Gaze of raccoons

Rhumba of rattlesnakes

Storytelling or unkindness of ravens

Crash or stubbornness of rhinos

Parliament, building, clamour
or storytelling of rooks

Hill of ruffs

Congress of salamanders

Fling of sandpipers

Family of sardines

Bed or nest of scorpions

Wreck of seabirds

Bob, crash, spring or rookery of seals

Shiver or school of sharks

Doading of sheldrakes

Escargatoire, rout or walk of snails

Den, nest, pit, bed or knot of snakes

Walk or wisp of snipe

Host of sparrows

Cluster or clutter of spiders

Scurry of squirrels

Murmuration or chattering of starlings

Fever of stingrays

Pack or trip of stoats

Muster or mustering of storks

Gulp or flight of swallows

Bevy, bank or herd of swans

Spring of teal

Mutation of thrushes

Streak or ambush of tigers

Knot, knab or nest of toads

Hover of trout

Rafter, gang or posse of turkeys

Pitying, piteousness or dule of turtledoves

Bale, turn or dole of turtles

Generation or nest of vipers

Venue of vultures

Kettle of vultures circling

Pod, school, mod, herd or gam of whales

Company of widgeon

281

Destruction of wildcats

Plump of wildfowl

Pack of wild or feral dogs

Pack or rout (when moving) of wolves

Fall of woodcocks

Descent of woodpeckers
Bed, clew, bunch or clat of worms

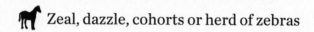 Zeal, dazzle, cohorts or herd of zebras

NEW SPECIES

The golden bum fly *Scaptia beyonceae* is a new species of horsefly discovered in north-east Queensland and named after the pop diva Beyoncé Knowles because of the dense patch of golden hairs at the tip of its abdomen and the year it was collected – 1981, the year of the singer's birth. It was not described until 2011.

In 2010, a new species of snub-nosed monkey *Rhinopithecus strykeri* discovered in the mountain forests of Burma was found to be 'allergic' to rain. Locally it's known as *myuk na tok te*, meaning 'monkey with the upturned nose' on account of its curious upturned snub nose. When rain falls it drops into its nostrils, making it sneeze, so at every downpour the monkeys tuck their heads between their knees. All the information about them comes from local hunters and trappers, for they are so endangered that no primatologist has seen one alive.

On the Philippines island of Luzon, a new dragon was discovered in 2009. Unlike the Komodo dragon, this monitor lizard *Varanus bitatawa* is a vegetarian – it eats fruit, especially *Pandanus* fruit – and lives in the trees. It grows to over 2m (6.6ft) long and is brightly coloured, the mottled green pattern on its body blending in with its leafy background. It lives in the north of the island where it is isolated from its nearest relative – Gray's monitor lizard *V. olivaceus* (which lives in the south of the island) – by three non-forested river valleys.

If you dislike cockroaches, look away now. A newly discovered South African cockroach *Saltoblattella montistabularis* has exceptionally long back legs, bulging eyes and moves like a grasshopper. It can leap forty-eight times its own body length, about 35cm (14 in.), in a single jump, with an acceleration of about 23 Gs, which is significantly more than a locust or grasshopper, which can only manage twenty body lengths. It lives in grasslands in the Table Mountain National Park, where it feeds, ironically, on grass-hopper droppings. It was first spotted in 2006 and described in 2010.

Two new species of springtails hold the record for the deepest-living underground invertebrates. In the summer of 2010, *Plutomurus ortobalaganensis* was found at a depth of 1,980m (6,496ft) and *Schaefferia profundissima* at 1,600m (5,249ft) in Krubera-Voronya cave, the world's deepest cave, on the eastern side of the Black Sea. They feed on fungi and decaying organic material.

In 2011, 'supergiant' amphipod crustaceans were found 7km (4.4 miles) down in the Kermadec Trench off the north-eastern tip of New Zealand's North Island. Shrimp-like amphipods are usually about 2–3cm (1in.) long, but the largest of these deep-sea amphipods was 34cm (13in.) long. As one of the scientists said at the time of the discovery, 'It's like finding a cockroach a foot long.'

A parasitic leech with unusually large teeth was found feeding on the nasal tissues of a girl who had recently bathed in waters of the eastern Amazon in Peru. The creature is little more than 44.5mm (1.75in.) long, but its eight very large teeth are each about 0.13mm (0.005in.) long and set in a single jaw. It was described in 2010 and given the name *Tyrannobdella rex,* meaning 'tyrant leech king'.

The world's smallest seahorse made itself known to dive guide Satomi Onishi, when he dived off Derewan Island in Indonesian Borneo in 2008, and he has the honour of having the little creature named after him. Satomi's seahorse *Hippocampus satomiae* is about 13.7mm (0.54in.) long, which is a fraction shorter than the previous record-holder, the 16mm (0.63in.) long *Hippocampus denise,* which was discovered on the gorgonian coral *Annella reticulata* off Banta Island, Indonesia, in 2003 and named after Denise Hackett who first found it.

The ghost slug *Selenochlamys ysbryda* was a surprising Welsh discovery, first at Brecon Cathedral in 2004, secondly in Caerphilly in 2006 and thirdly in a Cardiff garden in 2007. The pure white, nocturnal mollusc kills and eats earthworms using rows of blade-like teeth. Its scientific name is thought to be the first incorporating a Welsh word – *ysbruda*, meaning 'ghost'. Since being described, the ghost slug has been found near Swansea, Hay-on-Wye and Knowle near Bristol. It is thought to be an alien species, but how it came to be in Wales is a mystery.

The extraordinary *Opisthostoma vermiculum* snail, from Malaysia and described in 2008, looks like the brass section of an orchestra run over by a bus. Most gastropod molluscs have a single tight spiral on a single axis but this species has spirals on four different axes, which makes it the most convoluted snail on Earth.

A jet-black sea slug discovered in mangroves in the Gulf of Thailand in 2009 is amphibious. *Aiteng ater* secretes mucus over its body to prevent it from drying out, and it has a very odd diet for a sea slug, which usually grazes on algae: it feeds on the pupae of insects.

Many of the newly discovered species described above appear in the annual Top 10 New Species lists compiled by the International Institute for Species Exploration, Arizona State University.

AFTERWORD

The Frog with Self-cleaning Feet taps into the dedicated research of a great number of scientists working in laboratories or in the field all over the world but, if present trends continue, many of the animals they study may soon no longer be with us and their stories will come to an abrupt end. Populations of White's tree frog, which lends its name to this book, are holding up reasonably well, but many of its amphibian relatives are on the brink of extinction. Archey's frog *Leiopelma archeyi*, named after Sir Gilbert Archey (1890–1974), a former director of the Auckland Institute, is one of the world's rarest, smallest and most primitive frog species. It is critically endangered, its population in New Zealand having dropped by 80 per cent in ten years. The jewel-like golden toad *Bufo periglenes* of Costa Rica has already disappeared from its cloud forest home. In 1987, a scientist counted 1,500 of them, but in 1989 just one was sighted, and by 2004 it was declared extinct. Similarly, a search is on for the hula painted frog *Discoglossus nigriventer* from Israel, affected by a marsh-draining programme to curb malaria, the African painted frog *Callixalus pictus*, last seen in 1950 and never photographed, and the Mesopotamia beaked toad *Rhinella rostrata*, with its pyramid-shaped head, declared extinct in 1914. Could they be hiding somewhere? Alas, no.

Even with such a glum scenario, however, there is a hint of sunshine. Imagine the excitement when University of Manchester herpetologists, studying frogs in Costa Rica, chanced upon a tree frog *Isthmohyla rivularis* which was thought to have been extinct for at least two decades. Finding first a male in 2007 and then a female with eggs in 2008, this means the species has survived, against all the odds, and is breeding again when many other species have not. Fortunately, it also means we have something new to write about.